Gardener's Companion Series

The New Hampshire Gardener's Companion

An Insider's Guide to Gardening in the Granite State

Henry Homeyer

The
Globe
Pequot
Press

GUILFORD, CONNECTICUT

BT
14 95
2-5-07

The information in this book has been carefully researched. The author and publisher assume no responsibility for accidents happening to, injuries sustained, or any damage, loss, or inconvenience incurred by the reader as a result of following the information in this book. When using any commercial product, always read and follow label directions. Mention of a trade name does not imply endorsement by the publisher.

To buy books in quantity for corporate use or incentives, call **(800) 962–0973** or e-mail **premiums@GlobePequot.com.**

Text design by Casey Shain
Illustrations by Josh Yunger
Map by M. A. Dubé © Morris Book Publishing, LLC

Library of Congress Cataloging-in-Publication Data
Homeyer, Henry.
    The New Hampshire gardener's companion : an insider's guide to gardening in the Granite State / Henry Homeyer. — 1st ed.
        p. cm. — (Gardener's companion series)
    includes index.
    ISBN-13: 978-0-7627-4299-8
    ISBN-10: 0-7627-4299-2
    1. Gardening—New Hampshire. I. Title.
    SB453.2.N4H65 2007
    635.09742—dc22
                                                                    2006025676
Manufactured in the United States of America
First Edition/First Printing

To George Elliott Yunger,
my grandson, a gardener-to-be.
Even before the age of three, you have shown
your love of flowers, tomatoes, and carrots
straight from the garden.

Contents

Introduction

Gardening is America's favorite pastime. It's ahead of bowling, bee-keeping, and bird-watching. While it may be true that some New Hampshire residents log more hours at their televisions than in the garden, that's only because we have snow or cold for nearly half the year. Gardening here can be a challenge, that's for sure.

This book will offer you some advice about how to garden in the Granite State and how to get the most out of our short gardening season. I'm an organic gardener, so if you're looking for suggestions about what chemicals to spray on your apples or cabbages, this is not the book for you. But I will share with you some of what I've learned in more than fifty years of organic gardening, most of it right here in New Hampshire. I've been writing a gardening column for newspapers around New England since 1998, and I have learned a lot from other gardeners. I'd like to share some of that with you, too.

I started gardening in the early 1950s when my maternal grandfather, John Lenat, introduced me to the joys of playing with water and dirt, of studying earth-worms, and of eating ripe red tomatoes warmed by the summer sun. He didn't care if I got dirty and never complained if I just wanted to listen to his stories while he worked—instead of doing my weeding. I loved being with him, and he taught me to love the garden.

Grampy was an organic gardener long before it was popular. He made compost and worked it into his beds when other home gardeners were extolling the virtues of chemical fertilizers—then touted as the "modern" way to garden. We brought home buckets of chicken manure from the local egg farm, and he let me make "tea" for our tomatoes in an old wooden rain barrel. Instead of spraying his plants with chemicals, he picked off voracious bugs and put them in soapy water, a technique I still use.

I live in Cornish Flat, on the western edge of New Hampshire, about halfway up the state. Karen Woodbury (the light of my life, the baker of my pies) and I have just a couple of acres and an old wooden creamery built in 1888. But we have good soil, a small stream, and all the basic growing conditions one could want: full sun to full shade, wet to dry . . . and everything in between. And I am obsessed with trying to grow everything—from apples, arteme-sias, and artichokes to wildflowers, yuccas, and zucchinis.

It's my belief that gardening nourishes not only the body (with fresh vegetables), it also nurtures the soul. Had a hard day at work? Mad at (you pick) your teenager, wife, neighbor's ill-mannered dog? Get out in the garden. Pull weeds. Better yet, plant something. There is a primal urge wired into gardeners to plant things. Plant a six-pack of annual flowers and you'll feel better. Or pick some flowers and arrange them in a vase. You will feel like a new person, only vaguely resembling the grump who walked down to the garden.

Gardening is not all success, of course. Years ago striped cucumber beetles used to eat my cukes when they were in the two-leaf stage, gnawing them down to the ground. So I'd replant. And replant until the weather changed or the beetles found something else to eat. Some years I didn't get very many cucumbers because it was July before the seedlings got established, but I refused the "nuclear option"—pesticides. Then I learned about row covers. By stretching a layer of a thin agricultural fabric known as Reemay over the hill, I was able to physically prevent the beetles from get-ting to my plants. No poisons, and plenty of organic cucumbers.

This book is aimed at helping you deal with some of the challenges facing gardeners who reject chemicals.

This guide to gardening in New Hampshire is primarily based on methods that I have tried and found to work. It will also contain information I have learned from scientists and gardeners who have researched aspects of gardening outside my areas of expertise. But I've tried to keep this book user friendly: I have kept the science simple and have provided information that has real hands-on benefit to you, the gardener.

Thus, for example, I will share with you what research is going on to find nontoxic ways to control the lily leaf beetle (that gorgeous red beetle that is devastating lilies) or purple loosestrife (the purple flower that is taking over our wetlands). If I have used a word you don't know, you should find it in the glossary at the back of the book.

I went through the master gardener program offered by the University of New Hampshire Cooperative Extension in 1998, and the classes there filled in some of the gaps in my gardening education. The state extension service has offices in every county in the state and is an excellent resource for gardeners. This book will tell you where to go to get your soil tested, and how to get an answer *right now* about the black spots developing on your tomatoes.

From lawns and lilies to mulch and my nontoxic mole repellant, this book will provide useful information specifically geared to New Hampshire gardeners. Gardening should be fun, and I hope this book will also entertain you as you settle into an armchair midwinter or into an Adirondack chair on a hot summer afternoon.

Firm Foundations

Soils

There is no such thing as a gardener with a brown thumb. There *are*, however, gardeners with poor soil who *think* they have brown thumbs. To become a gardener with a green thumb, you need to improve your soil, as that is where success begins.

What's in Your New Hampshire Soil?

Soils are composed of three things: first, ground-up rocks that were largely created when the glaciers churned their way across New Hampshire and then retreated 10,000 years ago, grinding mountains into molehills—and into sand, silt, and clay. Running water and today's acid rain continue the process. Rock fragments typically amount to about half the volume of your soil.

Second, soil contains organic matter, which consists of the by-products and decomposed bodies of plants and animals. Dead leaves, cow manure, earthworm castings, or bacteria that have bitten the dust—all these count as organic matter. Good soil has 5 percent or more organic matter, while the average lawn's soil might have just 1 percent or less.

Third, topsoil contains air spaces. This last item amounts to nearly half the volume of good soil. Air spaces are important because they allow oxygen and water to reach the roots of plants. Plants absorb water, nutrients, and oxygen through their root hairs.

The soils of New Hampshire were mainly formed when the glaciers ground our granite bedrock into fine particles, says Steve

Hundley, New Hampshire's state soil scientist. The glaciers were more than 5,000 feet thick—so thick that there is even glacial soil on top of Mount Washington. The glaciers were dirty, Hundley notes, pushing up soil and grinding rocks into sand and gravel that became incorporated into the ice. As the glaciers melted, they left soil deposits—just as the dirty winter snow left by snowplows melts and leaves debris in the spring. Much of New Hampshire has relatively shallow soils that are dominated by that glacial residue of sand and gravel. Our soils, in general, are quite acidic, with unimproved soil pH values ranging between 4.0 and 5.5. (More on soil pH later in this chapter).

Where to Get Soil Maps

To learn about soil depth, type, and recommended agricultural uses for the soils in your neighborhood, visit http://soils.usda.gov. This site has information from soil maps prepared by the U.S. Department of Agriculture (USDA). Once at the Web site, select your state and county, then go to "soil data mart" or "web soil survey."

The Web site is not particularly user friendly, so you may prefer to call a real person at the National Resource Conservation Service (NRCS) in your county and ask for maps and surveys of your county. The NRCS is a part of the USDA, and staff members are more than happy to help you. You can even see an aerial photo of your property by visiting the county office of the NRCS. The maps are at a scale of 1:20,000, so 1 inch equals approximately 900 feet.

The soil surveys also contain records of precipitation, first and last frost dates, and monthly mean temperatures. The NRCS is in the process of making more information easily available at the USDA Web site cited above and should have it online by press time.

You can tell much about the history of your land by looking at the old stone walls, Hundley states. Rounded stones, by far the most common, are found in areas of glacial outwash—where melt water dumped sand, gravel, and rocks. These indicate soils of moderate depth and generally fast-draining soils containing sand. Walls built with jagged rocks are found where bedrock is close to the surface; pieces of the bedrock broke off after glacial times due to freezing and thawing. Areas with no old stone walls are probably glacial outwash plains. The plains are river valleys filled with glacial till; they are flat and contain deep soils that are relatively free of stones and boulders.

The richest soils in the state, Hundley explains, are in the Connecticut River valley. For thousands of years there was an ice dam in Windsor Locks, Connecticut, backing up what is now the Connecticut River into a huge lake called Lake Hitchcock. Clay and silt were slowly deposited in the lake over a long period of time, providing good soils. The Merrimac River valley is another area with good alluvial soils, even though it never was dammed up during the time of glaciers. In fact, alongside most streams and rivers throughout the state, and on the terraces bordering them, soils tend to have more silt and clay and less sand and gravel.

New Hampshire's seacoast region is yet another geomorphic region, according to Steve Hundley. The ocean rose as the glaciers melted, flooding land areas bordering the ocean up to what is now an elevation of about 200 feet. The ocean deposited marine silt and clay along the Portsmouth–Durham–Dover area. The clay was great for making bricks, but it is tough on gardeners.

Types of Soils

There are three basic soil types: sandy, silt, and clay. These three types of soil are mixed in different percentages throughout the state, creating many unique soil profiles.

Sandy soil is made of large mineral particles. Sandy soil lets water pass through quickly, draining off and going down to the sub-soil, leaving plants gasping for breath on hot, dry summer days. Minerals in a grain of sand are not available to plants. The grains need to be broken down—first physically, then dissolved with the help of acids in the soil, before their nutrients can be taken up by plant root hairs.

Silty soils have medium-size particles; silt holds water well but doesn't tend to stay waterlogged the way clay does. It is a major component of loam.

Loam is a mixture of sand, silt, clay, and organic matter. Good loam is what we all want but rarely what we have. If you are stuck with soils that aren't perfect, don't despair, soils can be improved—more on that later.

Clay soils, in contrast, are made of extremely fine mineral particles, each of which can be surrounded by water. Clay soils hold water, and they are often rich in minerals that plants need—and in forms that plants can use. Clay soils, also known as heavy soils, tend to stay wet, and some plants (such as fruit trees) don't do well when their "feet" are always wet. And when clay soils dry out, they can turn rock hard and be difficult for gardeners to work in or for plant roots to penetrate.

Humus is a chemically complex organic material that results from the breakdown of raw organic matter by microorganisms. Humus varies in composition, but it is a key ingredient in all good soils. Humus acts as a kind of piggy bank for plants, because water and mineral elements can attach themselves to electrically charged sites on humus particles. Water and minerals are released as needed.

A good soil is usually dark in color due to the presence of humus. If you go into the woods and look at the soil, it is usually dark from the humus that has been created by the decomposition of leaves over the years.

Other terms used to describe soil are *texture* and *tilth*. Texture refers to the particular blend of soil you have—the mixture of sand, silt, or clay—and how the particles are arranged. If you have lots of

Getting a Feel for Your Soil

Here are three tests you can perform to learn more about your soil.

1. Pick up a sample of your soil after a rainstorm when your soil is still moist, then rub the sample between your thumb and forefinger. What you are trying to do is determine the size of the particles. Sandy soil will have sharp grains that you can feel and see. Moist clay, on the other hand, is smooth and sticky when rubbed between your fingers. Silt is fairly smooth, but not sticky, and contains small grains you can feel. Most soils contain some of each of those three components.

2. Another way to judge your soil is to take a handful of soil and squeeze it into a ball. Open your hand. If the ball falls apart when you touch it lightly, you have a sandy soil. If the soil holds the impression of your hand like modeling clay and can be rolled into long cylinders between your hands, it is dominated by clay. Silt, like Goldilock's bed, is just right: neither too sticky nor too sandy. The longer the cylinder of wet soil you can roll out, the more clay present.

3. This test will give you a rough guide to the composition of your soil: Fill a widemouthed quart jar halfway with soil, add water until nearly full, shake it, and wait. Sand will fall to the bottom almost immediately. Silt (and some organic matter) will form a second layer within an hour or two. Some organic matter may float to the surface, depending on its moisture content. Clay will stay suspended in water for a day or two, keeping the water murky and dark. Once the water is clear, you should be able to see three layers and thus approximate the percentage of each in your soil.

If the three layers are all the same color, try draining the water, then use a spoon to sample the layers and feel their texture. Or try the test in a wide plastic container that will allow you to get your fingers on the sediments.

Buying Loam

Loam varies considerably in quality. If you intend to buy a few truckloads of it, I recommend checking it out first. After it has been dumped in your yard it is too late to complain. Bring a jug of water and try some of the tests mentioned in the "Getting a Feel for Your Soil" sidebar. If the "loam" is too sticky, it has too much clay in it, and that's not what you want. Remember, soils with good levels of organic matter are darker than average soils; wet soils are darker than dry ones, so check the loam on a dry day.

organic matter in the soil, and a nice mix of sand, silt, and clay, you should have good texture. Earthworms are great for creating good texture, as they exude compounds—gums and waxes—that hold bits of soil together. Humus, that dark stuff found in good topsoil, is also excellent for improving soil texture.

Tilth is a term that describes how well a soil holds water and allows air to pass through it. Tilth is determined in part by the soil structure. "Good tilth" describes a soil that is light and fluffy. You should be able to poke a screwdriver into the soil with little effort. If the screwdriver does not penetrate easily, your tilth is poor.

Be forewarned that tilth can be ruined by overeager gardeners. Spring in New Hampshire is usually long and wet, and we get impatient to start gardening. But if you walk in wet flower beds, or try to rototill the vegetable garden before the soil dries out, you can ruin its tilth. Test your soil with the squeeze test described in the "Getting a Feel for Your Soil" sidebar. Unless you can fragment the ball of soil with the tap of a finger, stay out of the garden.

Drainage

Plants have preferences just like you do. Some prefer dry soils, others thrive in wet ones, while most want soil that stays slightly moist but drains well after a rainstorm. Drainage depends on several things: soil type, soil texture, subsoil, and hilliness.

You can learn much about your soil by digging a hole 24 inches wide and deep. Try to keep the sides of the hole smooth and straight so that you can see the color of the soil. The topsoil, if it is rich in organic matter, should be a dark brown, and it might be just a couple of inches or (if you're lucky) as much as 6 or 8 inches deep. Next, you might have a layer of clay or sand or stones. Further down, near the bottom of the hole, look for gray- or white-colored soil. That discoloration indicates the water table, the level where soil stays saturated with water for much of the year. In the spring you may reach water before your hole is 2 feet deep.

You may hit bedrock or a layer of ledge before you dig 2 feet down, too. If your property is flat, or nearly flat, and you are on bedrock, your soil will not drain well—and that will affect what kinds of flowers and trees will do well for you. Big trees can blow over in high winds if roots can't go down to an adequate depth. Nut trees, in particular, want to send taproots down deep into the soil, and they are not a good choice for shallow soils.

Here's a simple test to learn about your soil's drainage: Dig a hole 2 feet diameter and 8 inches deep with sloping sides. Run water from the hose into the hole until it is full. Time how long it takes to drain. Sandy soils drain almost immediately. Heavy clay might take all day or longer. If it drains in an hour or two, you are in good shape. This test is not precise—it is affected by how much rain you have had in recent days: The wetter the soil, the longer it will take to drain off. But the test will give you a rough idea of the drainage conditions your plants face.

Soil Testing

Before you start your first garden, and every three or four years thereafter, it's a good idea to have your soil tested. A soil test can tell you the levels of important minerals, pH, soil type, and the amount of organic matter present in your soil. The University of New Hampshire Cooperative Extension offers this service for a nominal fee. Pay a little extra to get the "organic test," which should tell you how to remedy any deficiencies through the use of organic amendments. For more details, log on to http://extension .unh.edu/Agric/AGPDTS/SoilTest.htm. Or look in chapter 12, Resources, for the phone numbers of your local cooperative extension office. Give the office a call, and the staff will mail you all the information you need. Collecting the soil sample for the test is a simple process, and the tests are usually processed in a matter of days.

When is the best time to test your soil? According to state soil scientist Steve Hundley, fall is ideal. Most of New Hampshire soils are acidic, a condition that can be corrected by adding limestone. A soil test will recommend how much to add, but it takes time for the limestone to be dissolved and dispersed in the soil. A fall test will allow you to make the correction ahead of spring planting.

Soil pH and Plant Nutrients

The soil pH test measures the acidity or alkalinity of your garden soil and rates it on a scale of 1 to 14, with 7 being neutral. Different plants may need different pHs. Most plants do well in the range of 6.0 to 6.8, which is slightly acidic. If you have very acidic soil, say in the 4.5 to 5.5 range, most authorities would tell you to add ground limestone or wood ashes to sweeten the soil, bringing it closer to neutral. What's the big deal about soil pH? If the pH of your soil is too acidic (with a pH of 5.5 or less)—which is not uncommon in unimproved New Hampshire soils—the minerals calcium, phosphorus, and magnesium may be present in the soil but tied up and unavailable to plants. It's like being given a can of tunafish for dinner but no can opener to open it. Soils too sweet (with too high a pH, perhaps caused by the annual application of ashes without first testing the soil) may tie up phosphorus, iron, copper, zinc, boron, and manganese. When the soil pH is wrong, a plant may languish, turn yellow, or show other signs of nutrient deficiencies, even though the nutrients are in the soil. The plant just can't access them.

Be aware that acidic soil can also be a sign of a soil that has few minerals left to offer your plants. It works like this: Plants give off hydrogen ions from their root tips, trading the hydrogen ions for minerals in the soil—notably potassium, calcium, magnesium, iron, copper, zinc, and nickel. A pH test is actually a measure of hydrogen ions. If all the minerals just mentioned have been used up, there will be lots of hydrogen ions in the soil, and the test will indicate that it's highly acidic. Just adding limestone to the soil will not solve the problem. Yes, the pH will be better, but if the soil is depleted of minerals, your plants will still suffer. Adding organic matter or a bagged organic fertilizer will help replenish the soil with needed minerals. Your soil test will tell you what minerals need to be added.

Chemical Elements That Plants Need

We've just touched on a number of chemical elements that plants need but can't use if the pH is wrong. In fact, scientists have determined that plants require a total of sixteen or seventeen different chemical elements to live and thrive. Most of these chemical elements are found in compounds that chemically join two elements, such as the hydrogen and oxygen that make water. Thus, potassium in fertilizer is measured as potash, or, in scientist's terms, K_2O, and phosphorus is calculated as phosphate, or P_2O_5. These chemicals need to be broken down into two parts known as ions, which carry an electrical charge, in order to be used by plants. The breakdown process can be aided by the actions of microorganisms in a healthy soil.

Macronutrients

Let's first look at some of the more important elements—known as macronutrients—and how plants use them:

Carbon: Plants get their carbon from carbon dioxide, which is present in the air. They absorb it through stomata, or little holes on the underside of leaves. During the day, plants combine carbon dioxide and water through the process of photosynthesis to create sugars and carbohydrates that fuel all life processes in plants—and ultimately in animals.

Oxygen: Although oxygen is needed by plants for metabolic functions, plants are not as dependent on oxygen as animals are. Plants get oxygen through their roots, not through their leaves. A waterlogged soil, however, can eventually drown a plant because it deprives the plant of oxygen.

Carbon and oxygen can be considered "free" nutrients—gardeners don't need to provide them. The next three macronutrients—known as "the big three"—are often added to soils by gardeners.

Nitrogen: Plants generally absorb nitrogen from the soil in the form of ammonium or nitrate ions. Nitrogen is used by plants to make complex chemicals that we call proteins. Gardeners add nitrogen-containing fertilizers to stimulate green growth and to make plants get big fast. Too much nitrogen can keep plants from flowering or producing fruit, and high quantities can "burn" or even kill plants.

Phosphorus: This element comes in a variety of forms—naturally occurring forms derived from rocks, and other forms produced in chemical factories. Phosphate is important for developing good root systems and for promoting blooming, seed production, and fruits.

Potassium: It is important for developing good strong cell walls, which plants need to resist environmental stresses like drought and extremes of temperature, either hot or cold. Potassium is also involved in carbohydrate metabolism and cell division.

Three other elements are considered secondary macronutrients— necessary for plant health, but not in the same quantities as the big three.

Calcium is an important element in cell metabolism. It helps plants build proteins and take up nitrogen. Tomatoes, peppers, and squashes grown in low-calcium soils may develop blossom-end rot.

Magnesium is a part of the chlorophyll molecules needed for photosynthesis and is involved with enzyme use.

Sulfur is necessary for making proteins and fats. Most soils have sulfur, and it is also found in our acid rain. Sulfur makes onions pungent.

Micronutrients

Plants also need the following elements—called micronutrients—but in smaller amounts than the elements above. Be aware that not all fertilizers contain micronutrients. Natural, organic fertilizer will provide micronutrients but a conventional chemical fertilizer will not.

Iron is needed for making chlorophyll, enzymes, and proteins. An iron deficiency in rhododendrons can cause a yellowing of leaves known as interveinal chlorosis.

Chlorine is needed in photosynthesis and cell metabolism.

Manganese is also involved in making chlorophyll and is needed for making some vitamins. Peas are sensitive to low levels of manganese.

Zinc: Although not much zinc is needed, a little is required for building proteins and plant growth hormones, especially in corn and peaches.

Copper and **Boron:** Needed in even smaller quantities, these elements are important for various metabolic functions.

Molybdenum: Only a miniscule amount—two parts per million—of this metal is needed, but it is essential for protein synthesis and for the bacteria involved in nitrogen fixation.

Nickel: Small amounts are needed for plant metabolism.

How to Improve Your Soil

Okay, you have the results of your soil test in hand and it reveals a nutrient deficiency. What do you add to improve your soil?

First remember that Mother Nature knows best. Repeat that as needed, and as loudly as needed, especially if your spouse tries to convince you that all can be fixed with a good dose of chemical fertilizer. Compost and organic fertilizers provide all the nutrients and micronutrients needed by plants.

Chemical fertilizers—and by that I mean fertilizers created in factories using petroleum products and harsh chemical reactions—add only three useful elements: nitrogen, phosphorus, and potassium. Chemical fertilizers will not adjust the pH, add organic matter, or encourage beneficial microorganisms to live in your soil. In fact, some experiments have shown that chemical fertilizers can even make beneficial bacteria go dormant. Chemical fertilizers will not improve drainage or water retention, either, but there is something that will: adding compost and organic amendments. Let's look at what's available.

The Magic of Compost: Compost Helps Soil Structure

Adding compost improves soil structure and a soil's ability to hold moisture and drain well. Imagine a wire basket full of golf balls. Turn the hose on it and the water pours right through. That's how a sandy soil works. Now add lots of tiny little sponges (representing bits of compost), each smaller than a golf ball, and stir in. Turn on the hose. The wire basket still drains quickly, but it holds some water, just as sand will if you add compost.

Next imagine a bowl of dry baking flour. Add water, and it resists passing through. It puddles on the top. That's like a clay soil. If you add enough water and stir, you have a sticky mess. If it dries out, it's hard as a rock. Now imagine mixing in wheat germ, representing compost. Wheat germ has bigger particles than flour and helps to improve its texture. The resulting mixture is much easier to work with than straight flour.

Not only does compost improve soil structure, it also provides the full range of nutrients. True, compost is not high in nitrogen, the element that drives fast green growth. But a good compost has everything that a plant needs, and more. Compost feeds the microorganisms that work with plants, the bacteria and fungi that process raw materials and convert them into forms usable by plants. It is a slow, natural process.

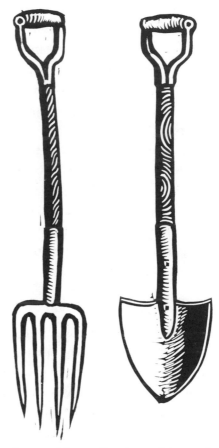

Adding Fertility with Organic Fertilizers

Soil tests rarely give recommendations for increasing nitrogen, as nitrogen levels change rapidly from day to day and week to week, depending on temperature, moisture levels, and other factors. If you have poor soil that is low in organic matter, or if your soil tests show low levels of phosphorus and potassium, you probably need to boost nitrogen levels, too. This can be done with application of bagged organic fertilizer. Organic fertilizers are made from plant and animal products such as seaweed, ground seashells, blood meal, and peanut hulls. Naturally occurring mineral products like rock phosphate and greensand are also present in them. These fertilizers provide the full range of elements needed by plants.

Karen and I have very high levels of organic matter in our vegetable garden, but we add a little bagged organic fertilizer at planting time with each transplant, stirring in a small handful of Pro-Gro (my organic fertilizer of choice) into a hole 12 inches or more across. This fertilizer provides extra nitrogen that gives my tomatoes and other plants a boost when starting out. In midsummer I scratch some in next to my carrots to give them

Don't Turn Your Garden into Concrete!

If you have a heavy clay soil, don't add sand, thinking that will solve the problem—you may end up with something like concrete. A clay-and-sand mixture can turn hard as a rock when it dries out. Instead, add in *lots* of compost.

a boost. And I add some each time I plant a perennial, as I know it adds lots of micronutrients in addition to the "big three."

Organic fertilizers depend on microorganisms to convert them into forms that can be used by plants. Unlike chemical fertilizers, a big rainstorm won't dissolve your organic fertilizers, so they won't end up in our water systems. They are broken down into usable forms more quickly in hot weather—when they are needed most.

Applying Other Soil Amendments

Ground limestone provides calcium and helps to neutralize acids in the soil. If the soil is too acidic, some minerals will be tied up and not readily available to your plants. If you buy dolomitic limestone, you also get magnesium, another element needed by plants. If your soil is very acidic, say at the pH 4.5 to 5.0 range, you will not be able to bring the pH up to the optimal 6.0 to 6.8 range in one year.

The UNH Cooperative Extension will suggest how much limestone to add when you get the results of your soil test. You might want to get an inexpensive pH test kit at your local garden center and test yearly until your soil approaches neutral. There are several forms of limestone: pelletized, ground, and hydrated or slaked. The

Organic Fertilizers Available in New Hampshire

These organic fertilizers, and perhaps others, are available throughout the state. Look for the word "organic" on the bag. Some others will say "all natural," which is good, but not the best.

Pro-Gro: Made in Bradford, Vermont, from seaweed, fish-meal, ground oyster shells, rock phosphate, whey, blood meal, compost, and agricultural by-products like peanut meal. It is my fertilizer of choice. It's a 5-3-4 fertilizer, with about one-third of the nitrogen immediately available and the rest released slowly, as are most of the other ingredients. The Web site, www.norganics.com has many excellent technical reports for advanced gardeners.

Blue Seal: Their Safe 'N Simple Plant Food is a 5-5-5 made from soy, alfalfa, and fish meals. It is readily available around the state wherever Blue Seal feeds are sold.

Espoma: This company makes a variety of fertilizers from organic ingredients. Plant-Tone, the all-purpose fertilizer, is a 5-3-3. Espoma fertilizer bags, unlike those of most other brands, list guaranteed content of many of the micronutrients needed by plants.

What Do Those Numbers on a Bag of Fertilizer Mean?

They list the contents of the bag as percentages of total weight. The first number is always nitrogen, the second phosphorus, the last potassium. Thus 5-10-5 contains 5 percent nitrogen usable to plants by weight, 10 percent phosphorus, and 5 percent potassium. Chemical fertilizers contain filler to help keep gardeners from burning the roots of their plants and to make the fertilizer easier to spread. Organic fertilizers are made from plant and animal by-products and include other nutrients to fill up the bag.

latter two are not for gardeners, but any limestone you buy at a garden center should be fine.

Wood ashes: Like limestone, wood ashes sweeten the soil, making it less acidic. If a soil recommendation is for ten pounds of limestone per thousand square feet of garden space (a plot 20 x 50 feet), you would need about twice as much wood ash to get the same effect. It is very fine, and you should be careful not to inhale it—apply it on a day with no wind, and wear a mask. No particulate matter is good for your lungs. Wood ashes act faster than limestone because the texture is so fine. They also are a good source of potassium.

Rock phosphate, black rock phosphate, colloidal phosphate: These are all good forms of phosphate for organic gardeners. They are derived from rocks and release phosphorus to plants slowly, over a multiyear period—up to five or seven years. Rock phosphate is the slowest to be taken up by plants, colloidal phosphate the fastest. Rock phosphate also contains 33 percent calcium and has about 20 percent of the neutralizing effect of limestone. Colloidal phosphate is the best choice for sandy soil as it also contains clay, which can help to bind sand particles and increase its ability to hold on to nutrients and water.

Phosphate attaches itself to soil particles on contact and thus does not migrate through the soil like nitrogen fertilizers—unless abnormally high levels of phosphate are present. When planting trees or shrubs, I do not use nitrogen-containing fertilizers, but I am always sure to add rock phosphate in the hole to get it down deep where it will be used. Manure or composted manure from dairy barns may be very high in phosphate, even to the point of leaching into streams if you use too much, so be moderate and get your soil tested if you use a lot of fresh manure.

Greensand and other sources of potassium: Greensand is another good natural additive to soil. It comes in a fifty-pound bag primarily sold as an additive to provide potassium, but it also contains magnesium, iron, calcium, phosphorus, and some thirty different micronutrients. It comes from an ancient undersea deposit in

New Jersey. The primary ingredient is a mineral known as glauconite, an iron potassium silicate compound.

New Hampshire soils are more likely to be low in potassium than any other major ingredient, says Tom Buob, an extension educator for UNH Cooperative Extension. Greensand is an excellent source of potassium, but wood ashes are rich in potassium, too—and cheaper.

A New Hampshire company is now selling its own brand of soil amendment known as Heart & Soil pH Plus made from ash produced at wood-fired power plants. It contains 4.4 percent potassium and 11 percent calcium, about a third the amount of calcium of limestone. (Visit www.heartnsoil.com for a list of garden centers that sell it.)

Rock dust or rock flour: I've been adding finely ground rock powders to my soils for the past five years. I get it from places that cut granite for tombstones. Rock dust is sold commercially in bags as Azomite, which contains "minerals from A to Z" according to the ads. Not often found in garden centers, Azomite may be purchased from seed companies like Fedco of Maine (see chapter 12). Garden centers that sell Pro-Gro can order Azomite from the maker of Pro-Gro.

Fine rock powders seem to energize plants, getting them to start off faster. I've particularly observed this with my potatoes. Applied late in the season, it has appeared to help in the production of my sweet peppers. My observations are anecdotal, not scientific, however. Years of controlled tests are needed.

When I interviewed retired professor Ward Chesworth of the University of Guelph in Ontario, he postulated that the fine rock powders may provide some of the trace elements that the glaciers would provide—the next time they return. I liked his metaphor that farmers "have been making tea with the same bag for 10,000 years." Granite dust may supply minerals that scientists have yet to identify as important.

How much rock dust to use? I use about fourteen pounds per

100 square feet, but some other gardners use three times that amount. I'm intrigued by the stuff, in part due to an article I read about the farmers in the Hunza Valley of Pakistan who irrigate their crops with "glacial milk"—water from a glacier that is high in fine rock particles. They routinely live to be over one hundred years old, and there are those who attribute the Hunza farmers' longevity to the minerals in their food. Go to www.remineralize.org for more information.

Final Thoughts

What's the key to success in the garden? Improving your soil. Add organic matter and good compost. Get a soil test done. Stay away from chemical fertilizers; they never provide the full range of minerals needed by plants nor do they improve soil texture or structure. And lastly, be patient. It takes years to get your soil to the quality you'd like to have. But you will get there—if you keep at it.

Growing Seasons

New Hampshire's growing seasons vary considerably throughout the state and change from year to year. Perennial flowers, trees, and shrubs wake up and start growing in April after their long winter's nap, but most annual flowers and vegetables aren't able to survive and thrive until the weather warms in May and June. Even frost-hardy veggies like peas don't grow much until the soil warms up and the sun has strength. However, there is much a gardener can do to stretch the growing seasons and to keep tender plants happy despite the cold.

Determining Your Hardiness Zone

New Hampshire spans three USDA Hardiness Zones: 3, 4, and 5. The best way to decide what zone you live in is to keep track of the coldest temperatures each winter at your particular site—or talk with a neighbor who has done so. Keep in mind that temperatures vary from year to year, so you can't buy trees or perennials just based on what last winter was like.

Hardiness zones are important considerations when buying perennial flowers, shrubs, and trees: They limit what you can grow. Even a few days at minus 30 degrees may kill your 'Reliance' peach tree or kousa dogwood. If you're new in town, ask a neighbor how

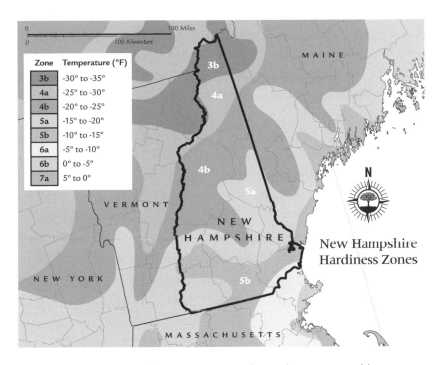

Zone	Temperature (°F)
3b	-30° to -35°
4a	-25° to -30°
4b	-20° to -25°
5a	-15° to -20°
5b	-10° to -15°
6a	-5° to -10°
6b	0° to -5°
7a	5° to 0°

New Hampshire
Hardiness Zones

The USDA Hardiness Zone map shows the average coldest
temperatures in New Hampshire. Take these zone ranges with a grain
of salt. Due to the presence of microclimates, zones can vary
tremendously even within a town.

cold it gets, or talk to the folks at your local family-run gardening
center—they know what survives here.

Most of the state is in Zone 4, which means that during an
average winter—and we all know there is no such thing—the temperature in your garden will go down to at least minus 20, but no
colder than minus 30. Near the Canadian border and in the White
Mountains temperatures can get even colder: The average coldest
temperatures are 30 to 40 degrees below zero, qualifying as Zone 3,
even though these extreme temperatures may occur only for a few
days each year. In the cities, along the seacoast, and in the southern parts of the state, gardeners only have to endure 10 to 20
degrees below zero, which is considered Zone 5.

Weather Records for New Hampshire

The two key dates for vegetable gardeners are the last frost in the spring and the first frost in the fall. But where do you get this information?

The state does not have any easy way for gardeners to access weather records for recent years. The county soil surveys prepared by the USDA do include weather information, but it is outdated. My Sullivan County soil survey, for example, has weather records for 1951–79, which is interesting but not necessarily relevant today. According to my soil survey, one year in ten the last spring frost is later than June 3, and five years in ten it is later than May 20. That sounds about right. The records show that one year in ten the first autumn frost is earlier than September 13, and five years in ten it is earlier than September 18. I've seen years where frost did not come until mid-October, and once, in 1982 or 1983, when the first frost was the third week in August for some gardeners in town.

The World Wide Web offers information about New Hampshire weather and climate. The weather Web site www.rss weather.com/climate has data for Concord from 1971 to 2000, including average high and low temperatures, average monthly precipitation, and the percentage of possible sunshine per month. The National Weather Service in Gray, Maine, covers New Hampshire and posts data for several towns in the state. Go to www.weather.gov/climate/xmacis.php?wfo=gyx and you can find first and last frost dates for the past year and for the 1971–2000 period, plus lots of other information.

Data from the National Weather Service indicate that there is an average growing season of 120 days for frost-sensitive crops like tomatoes in my county. In 2005 there were 153 frost-free days, according to their records.

The point of all this weather information is to learn your first and last frost date. Each garden plot is different, so averages are only a starting point. I wait to plant frost-sensitive plants in the garden until any chance of frost has passed. Cold air slides downhill, and my site is at the bottom of a hill, so I get frost even when my uphill neighbors don't. In my Zone 4 garden, the last spring frost is usually in late May, but I wait until around June 5 to plant things that might be killed or injured by frost. That allows the ground to warm up more, too. Heat-loving annual plants don't grow much in cold soil.

Microclimates

Even on your own land the temperature and growing conditions can vary considerably. My vegetable garden often gets frost when the flower beds around the house do not. That's because the house is 15 feet higher in elevation and also acts as a reservoir of warmth, radiating heat at night.

Will Your Veggies and Flowers Survive a Light Frost?

No: Basil, beans, cilantro, cukes, dill, eggplants, melons, peppers, pumpkins, all kinds of squash, and tomatoes. All annual flowers are frost sensitive, but some will survive light frosts.

Yes: Artichokes, broccoli, cabbage, carrots, cauliflower, celery, chives, corn, garlic, greens, horseradish, kale, leeks, lettuce, onions, oregano, parsley, parsnips, peas, spinach, Swiss chard, thyme, and turnips. Perennial flowers are generally not frost sensitive, and some bulbs like snowdrops will push up flower stalks through frozen soil and survive repeated nights of temperatures in the twenties.

Potato vines will get killed by frost, but the spuds won't get hurt. Rosemary is a perennial in Mediterranean climates and will survive light frosts, but it needs to come inside to winter over.

Cold air is denser than warm air—the reverse of the principle used to fly hot-air balloons—so it tends to flow downhill. My land has hills on two sides, creating a valley; lots of cool air fills my garden in spring and fall, bringing frosts to us earlier than others in town.

Exposed rock, particularly if dark in color, will absorb heat in the day and radiate it at night. I sometimes place black stones around the base of heat-loving plants like eggplants to help them stay warmer at night.

The top of a hillside, though in full sun, may not be the best place for a garden if it is constantly windy; the wind will cool and dry the plants all summer long. A barn, a hedge, or a wooded area may spill some shade onto your plants yet encourage them to grow better by blocking the wind.

In New Hampshire the best exposure for warmth-loving plants is on a gentle hillside facing the southeast. The spring sun will warm it first, and a slope helps to drain away excess moisture, an important factor in getting our soils ready to plant. North-facing slopes are poor choices for growing much of anything but hay or forest.

Sun and Shade

This far north the sun changes its arc considerably as seasons change. Before you plant an orchard or create an extensive flower bed, you should keep records of the patterns of sun and shade over the course of a year. The number of hours of direct sun is important to your plants, and a row of evergreens will shade your plot differently in April than it will in August.

Full sun is most important in spring, to warm the soil, and in midsummer when your plants do the bulk of their growing. It doesn't matter so much if the house shades a flower bed in early spring or late fall—your plants are less active then anyway.

Extending Your Growing Seasons

There are many ways to extend the New Hampshire growing seasons, including such things as warming the soil, choosing plant varieties that do well in cold climates, and even building simple hoop houses or cold frames to protect plants. Let's look at your options more closely.

Get an Early Start

Impatient to get going in the spring? One of the best ways to get an early start is to prepare your vegetable beds in the fall. That way you can sneak in a few seeds or frost-hardy plants without ruining soil structure by working in wet soil in spring.

Even if the air temperatures are warm in the spring, wet soils don't warm up quickly. And you need both: warm days and warm soil. Heat-loving plants prefer soil temperatures to reach 50 degrees before being planted.

In the fall, clean up the vegetable garden of that year's weeds and dead plants. Add compost to the beds and work it in. Then hill up the soil in beds 30 inches wide with walkways in between. No need to use planks to contain the soil, just mound it up about 6 inches above the paths and work in some compost. These raised beds will warm up more easily and drain faster than flat soil.

On a sunny day in spring, you can heat up the soil by stretching clear plastic sheeting over your beds. Pin it down with agricultural staples, rocks, planks, or soil so that it won't blow it away or let cool air in. Clear plastic heats the soil better than black plastic because the sun goes right through it and directly warms your soil. Black plastic will eventually warm the soil, however, and it is used by some gardeners to keep weeds from germinating. I've never kept plastic down for more than a week, but your needs may be different. Be prepared to experiment.

I've measured temperatures above 100 under clear plastic on a sunny day when the air temperature was only 65 degrees. This

When Can I Start My Vegetable Garden?

It might be exciting to get outside and plant things in mid-April, and some New Hampshire gardeners do, but there's not much point to planting early if your soil is wet and cold. Early crops that grow in cold weather include spinach, peas, and hardy lettuces. But if you plant too early, seeds can rot—and nothing grows very much when the soil is 40 degrees or cooler. Early to mid-May is a safe planting date for those cold-weather crops most years. Ask an old-timer in your town for advice.

Remember: Don't rototill the soil or walk on areas you will be planting when the soil is wet, or you may damage the soil structure and tilth of your garden.

method, called solarization, will also cook any annual weed seeds that have already germinated. A few days of solarizing the soil doesn't raise the temperature much, but it helps. Try not to disturb the soil when planting seeds in the warmed soil, as soil deeper down will still be plenty chilly.

A new type of plastic sheeting was developed at the University of New Hampshire by professor Brent Loy. Called IRT mulch, this plastic allows heat-producing infrared rays to pass through and reach the ground but keeps out visible light, thus suppressing weeds. It's available from Fedco Seeds or Johnny's Selected Seeds (see the resources in chapter 12).

You can extend the growing season in the fall, too. I refuse to let my tomatoes, basil, cucumbers, and squash plants get turned black and mushy by a September frost. I know that there will be plenty of warm weather still ahead, so I go out and cover them every clear night when frost is predicted or when the temperature is less than 50 degrees at 5:00 P.M. I use old bedspreads, sheets, plastic sheeting, and blue tarps. I use rocks and bricks to keep the covers in place, particularly if it's windy. I like to get the covers in place by 5:00 P.M., or earlier, before the air gets too cold, so that the covers hold in the daytime heat soaked up by the earth before that heat dissipates.

There are times when I forget to cover, or when the clouds — which serve as a kind of giant blanket—move off after I've gone to bed, and I wake up to frost on the garden. All is not lost: I take the hose and wash off the frost, which, for many vegetables, will give them a reprieve. That, of course, depends on how cold it got, too. A frost of 31 degrees is survivable for many things, but a frost of 28 degrees is not.

How long can you extend the gardening season? You can make it as long as you want it to be, within reason. If you start spinach on May 1 and still have carrots and beets in the ground on Thanksgiving Day, as we often do, your growing season is about 200 days. But for cold-sensitive crops like tomatoes and pumpkins, the best you can do in New Hampshire is more like 100 to 120 days—and sometimes less than that.

Pick the Right Varieties

Select varieties of vegetables and flowers that are said to do well in cold climates.

Then, to maximize your crops, select at least some varieties with the shortest number of days possible to harvest. An heirloom 'Brandywine' tomato will take seventy-eight days or more from seedling to sandwich, while 'Early Girl' (a patio-type tomato) requires only sixty days; my favorite cherry tomato, 'Sun Gold', takes only fifty-seven days—three weeks earlier than Brandywines! I plant several varieties each year so that I get an early crop, a batch of heirlooms with their extra-sweet flavor, and a crop of the bigger tomatoes that generally take longer to mature. This way if an early frost catches me unprepared and I lose my plants, the year is not lost for tomatoes.

Some seed catalogs or packets don't tell all they should. For starters, they *assume* that gardeners will know that a tomato labeled "sixty-five days to harvest" means *sixty-five days from transplant*. They *assume* you know that vegetables that are never started indoors (like carrots or beets, for example) are labeled with the number of days from planting seeds *outdoors* to harvest. Read the fine print so you won't be disappointed by planting tomato, pepper, or eggplant seeds outdoors. In New Hampshire they won't succeed that way.

Give Your Early Plants Sweaters

You can protect early plantings from frost by covering them with spun-bonded polypropylene agricultural fabric, also known as row covers. The best known of the products is Reemay, but many types are now available, each differing in weight and ability to let light pass through (70 percent to 90 percent light transmission fabrics are available). Reemay can be placed right over the soil and pinned down after planting or draped over wire hoops to create tents or tunnels. Unlike clear plastic, row cover fabric breathes, allowing temperatures to moderate and moisture to pass through. The heaviest of row covers can protect frost-sensitive plants down to 26 degrees. Agribon is another reputable brand.

Row covers are also great for protecting your tasty young plants from insect pests like striped cucumber beetles and flea beetles. I keep Reemay over cukes and squashes until they

Does the Full Moon Accompany the First Frost?

Common New Hampshire lore says that the last frost of the spring coincides with the full moon. But is that true? Gardener Sally Wellborn of Cornish kept records of frost dates for more than 20 years. When her son, Gwyn Gallagher, was a college student, he decided to test the theory. He took his mother's records and correlated them with the phases of the moon over all those years. He determined that the moon does *not* affect the temperature.

start to blossom, then I remove it—row covers keep the pollinating insects out as well as the pests.

Another type of plant sweater is a product known as a Wall-o-Water, available at most garden centers and in many seed catalogs. This device encloses plants in an 18-by-18-inch plastic cylinder that holds three gallons of water in plastic baffles. During the day the Wall-o-Water absorbs heat, storing it in the water; heat radiates out at night. During cold times the top can be drawn in, creating a toasty tepee. I've used them, and they do work. The maker claims it will protect frost-sensitive plants down to 16 degrees. They are also good for warming the soil if you set them out a week or two before planting. As tomato plants get bigger, the Wall-o-Water can be opened up to let the plants emerge. A Wall-o-Water should last several years.

Hot caps are another way to protect plants in the spring. The cheapest are homemade: Cut the bottom out of gallon milk jugs and place them over new transplants. Take off the cap to keep excessive heat from building up during the day, and put the cap back on at night.

Build a Simple Greenhouse or Hoop House

Owning a simple unheated greenhouse or hoop house is a great way to extend the seasons and to grow heat-loving plants faster than their counterparts living outside in New Hampshire's often chilly weather. Chilly nights—in the forties, say—are discouraging to things like peppers, so I grow these heat lovers in a hoop house I built myself.

Commercial greenhouses with aluminum frames glazed with flat panels of 4- or 6-mil polycarbonate "glass" are readily available but a bit pricey for my budget. Growers Supply (see chapter 12) sells many different models, some starting under $1,000. Gardener's Supply in Burlington, Vermont (see chapter 12) sells a variety of them through its catalog, but you can also go to Burlington to look at greenhouses in some seasons—call first to be sure. Gardener's Supply even has one that arrives on a flatbed truck fully assembled, ready to set in place.

If you enjoy building things and are a decent weekend carpenter, you can construct your own hoop house for just a fraction of the price. I built one that is 10 feet long, 8 feet wide, and tall enough to walk in. It took me about eight hours to build and cost me $100, not counting the materials I had kicking around the barn. Those included an old aluminum storm window, a screen door with a ruined screen, and a big sheet of used greenhouse plastic. See the sidebar "How to Build Your Own Hoop House" for details about my project.

I start spinach and other early greens each fall in the hoop house. They get established then go dormant until the ground thaws in March or April. Most of them start growing again (though I lose a few). Later, come summer, I grow peppers inside the hoop house where it is hotter and where I can control the amount of water they get—they don't like wet soil, having originated in Mexico. I also plant a few tomatoes in the hoop house each year, including one heirloom that takes forever outdoors but produces earlier in the hoop house.

Use Hot Boxes and Cold Frames

Gardeners have been cheating Jack Frost each spring for generations with cold frames. My grandfather built wooden boxes for early vegetables, covering them with recycled wood-framed storm

How to Build Your Own Hoop House

I built my on-a-budget hoop house by first selecting a site that was flat and in full sun. I established a straight line with a string and two stakes. Next I took 2-foot-long pieces of ½-inch rebar (steel rod used to reinforce concrete) and drove it 12 inches into the ground every 2 feet along the string. Rebar is sold in long lengths, but the lumberyard has a machine for cutting it, so I asked them to cut it into 2-foot sections. I angled the bars just ever so slightly out—away from what would become the interior of the hoop house.

Next I used a framing square, tape measure, and an 8-foot 2x4 to establish another line parallel to the first and 8 feet away from it. I set up another string and drove rebar along that line opposite the first row of rebar.

I purchased twelve 10-foot lengths of 1-inch diameter PVC pipe, the kind that electricians use. I glued these together in pairs and let the cement cure for fifteen minutes before proceeding. Then I slipped one end of what was now a 20-foot pipe over a piece of rebar that was sticking out of the ground, and I gently bent the PVC pipe over, creating a hoop. I slipped the other end of the pipe over the rebar opposite it, 8 feet away. I repeated this five times, and the basic structure was in place. It looked like the real thing! (Or the ribcage of a great blue whale.)

I then stabilized the hoops by attaching three 10-foot lengths of wood strapping (1½-by-¾-inch lumber) to the plastic pipe. I did this by screwing right through the wood into the ribs—the plastic pipes—using a portable drill and 1½-inch galvanized Phillips screws. I attached strapping on either side of the hoop house 30 inches above ground and parallel to it, and then I added a piece on top, right down the middle.

The end walls needed to be framed up next: one end for a door, the other for a window that would allow me to regulate temperatures by opening and closing it. But first I

continued

took a hoe and scraped out a trench where the walls would stand. I made it about 8 inches wide by 6 inches deep and filled it with crushed stone, making sure it was level. One should never use pressure-treated wood near food crops, but untreated wood rots quickly if it's in contact with soil and water. The gravel allows the wood to dry out and last longer. You can also paint your 2x4s with linseed oil to prolong their useful life.

I put a 2x4 on top of the gravel from one side of the hoop house to the other and screwed through the pipe on each side with a 3½-inch screw. This served as the base for the wall. Then I framed up a door frame for the screen door I intended to use. I allowed an extra ¾ inch on each side to keep the door from jamming if the wood swelled. I attached the uprights to the plastic hoops with plumber's strap. This comes as a roll of flexible metal strap an inch wide that is full of holes for screws. I wrapped straps around the hoop, then screwed the straps to the 2x4s.

At the other end of the hoop house, I framed an opening for an aluminum storm window, the kind with two pieces of glass that slide up and down on tracks. I positioned the window up as high as possible so I could vent heat on hot days.

New Hampshire winds are strong and I didn't want to see the hoop-house plastic blown off. I needed to attach it firmly with battens, or wood slats, not only on the top and sides but also on the ends. So I took a jigsaw and shaped 1-by-8-inch boards to fit the curve of the hoops, nailed them to the 2x4 uprights, and attached them with plumber's strap to the hoops.

The next job is a two-person task that should be done on a day with little wind: fitting the plastic sheeting over the hoop house. I used a piece 30 feet long and 25 feet wide, which allowed for plenty of extra on all sides. Two of us pulled it up and over the hoop house. I fixed the plastic in place with three more 10-foot lengths of strapping, sandwiching it between these and the strapping already in

place. I further secured the plastic by screwing battens to the 1x8s on the end walls and on the vertical 2x4s there.

The storm window went in place easily. I wrapped the screen door with plastic and added a latch to keep it from blowing open.

The hoop house has been remarkably successful. It has held up to winter winds and snow that didn't always slide off. I did brace the end walls with 2x4s, each set at a 45-degree angle between the wall and ground inside.

windows. On sunny days he propped the lids open, and then closed them at night. Nowadays you can buy premade cold frames for under $100 that utilize sheets of twin-wall polycarbonate "glass" and aluminum frames.

I have built hot boxes that use fermenting horse manure to provide heat to a cold frame. Hot boxes have largely fallen out of favor, perhaps because good hot manure is hard to find. Horse barns now use so much bedding (and they clean stalls so often) that there isn't enough manure mixed in to ferment well.

To build a hot box, dig a hole the size of your desired hot box and a foot deep. Line the sides with 2-inch-thick foam insulation to keep the heat from dissipating laterally. Fill it with steaming-hot horse manure. Then add 4 inches of topsoil to plant in. The bottom heat from the manure is great for germinating seeds and growing plants. The lettuces I planted in mid-April germinated quickly and grew well.

One word of caution: If the ground is too cold, the bacteria fermenting and producing the heat can go dormant. That happened to me once. I had to dig out all the manure and bring in another batch, which tempered my enthusiasm for starting earlier than mid-April.

Helping Plants Survive Tough Winters

By the end of February, I feel like one of those penguins in a French documentary as I walk the dog on cold nights in my many layers of clothing. Some of my plants are bundled up, too.

Trees and shrubs: Here's what I do: In early January I wrap an old blanket around any young tree that is not well established, keeping the blanket in place with a nylon strap. Then I spread some hay around the base to protect the roots from extreme cold. For small shrubs and roses, I crisscross cut evergreen boughs over and around a plant, then fluff up some hay and spread it on top. I've overwintered tea roses that way, which most New Hampshire gardeners assert are "definitely not hardy here."

Here's my theory: It's not just the cold that kills things, it's the wind, too. Whenever we get a strong subzero wind for a couple of days, I lose woody plants—or their buds. Fruit buds on my blueberries and blackberries get burned off by cold winds but survive the cold if it's less windy.

It's also my theory that the first three years of a tree's life are the most critical. Once a plant is well established, it'll do better than youngsters. So I pamper young trees and shrubs during the three-year break-in period. After that? They have to fend for themselves.

Perennials: I regularly grow perennials that are rated Zone 5 or warmer in my Zone 4 garden by finding just the right spot to plant them. A vigorous plant that has good soil, good drainage, and the right amount of sunshine is more likely to survive than one that is just limping along. Soil pH is also a key to success for some plants.

If your neighbor can grow lavender, for example, you can, too. Ask what she has done, and look at the site and soil. Consult a

Soil Thermometers

Soil thermometers have steel probes attached to a dial that reads the temperature. I use mine in the spring to see when the soil has reached the elusive 50-degree mark that tells me it's okay to plant warm-weather crops. I use it to see if my compost pile is heating up properly. One winter when we had more than 3 feet of snow on the ground, I shoveled a spot in the vegetable garden to see if snow was the insulation it is claimed to be. It is. Only the top inch of soil was frozen, and 4 inches down the temperature was 39 degrees.

good reference text that tells about soil, moisture, and shade preferences for the particular plant you want to grow. It might mean that at planting time you have to improve drainage and sweeten the soil by adding limestone. Given all that, sometimes I fail anyway. I'm willing to try a perennial three times, and then, as in baseball, if I fail, "It's out!"

Final Thoughts

New Hampshire's weather can be harsh and is often unpredictable—which, we are regularly told, builds character and keeps us on our toes. Perhaps. I like to say that 30 below keeps out the riffraff. And that goes for insect pests, too. Some of the insects that devastate southern New England plants are absent or rare in our climate. A good cold winter is helpful in keeping their numbers down. So if the frost gets your squash before you were ready, remember that there's a good side to the cold. And there's always next year.

Water

As a little boy I loved to run through the sprinkler in the heat of August, reveling in the sensations of cool water and wet grass. It was almost as much fun as squirting my sister with the hose and being squirted back.

Many towns and cities these days have outlawed watering lawns and gardens, or at least when green things need it the most—the dog days of the summer. Healthy plants with deep root systems can withstand considerable drought, and there is much one can do to help plants survive dry times. This chapter will discuss how much water your plants need, and we'll review various watering and mulching options that can keep your garden lush in dry times.

How Much Water Do Your Plants Need?

New Hampshire is blessed with fairly regular precipitation, averaging 3 to 4 inches per month year-round. According to National Weather Service data, New Hampshire in the past ten years has averaged as much as 7.55 inches per month in the fall of 2005, or as little as 2.57 per month in the fall of 2001. Summer months over the past century have averaged 3.85 inches per month.

Averages mean little, of course, if it's 90 degrees outside and your newly planted tomatoes are wilting. Watering can be critical for the survival of your plants. Water is the largest single component of plant tissue, and an adequate supply of H_2O is necessary for success in the garden.

That said, asking me the question "How much water do my plants need?" is a little like asking "How much should I feed my dog?" without telling me the age, breed, and exercise habits of the dog. Let's get more specific.

Vegetables, annuals, and perennials: The rule of thumb for vegetables and annual flowers is that they need 1 inch of water per week—either from rain or from your hose. Some well-established perennial flowers might not suffer from a month of dry weather, but young tomato transplants might not survive three days of blazing sun without getting a drink. Part of being a good gardener is being observant—and checking your garden regularly to see if plants need your help.

Trees: Mother Nature does a pretty good job of taking care of trees in the forest, and she will do so for you, too. But *young* trees are different. They need to be watered every week unless you are in a very rainy time. A brief shower will not do the job.

Five gallons of water per week per tree is best. If you are using a hose attached to a watering wand, time how long it takes to fill a five-gallon pail. For me, it's about a minute, but that depends on water pressure. Then watch the second hand or count to yourself as you water each tree. You'd be surprised how long it takes to deliver five gallons. Distribute water in a 3-

What Time of Day Should You Water?

Each gardener has a theory on the ideal watering time. Some say watering should be done early in the morning so that the sunshine will evaporate water off leaves, reducing the possibility of fungal disease. Others say water in the evening, so that moisture can soak down deep into the soil and not evaporate so quickly. Me? I say water when you have the time and your soil is dry. Pay attention to how your plants respond, and decide for yourself. It's not rocket science.

to 4-foot circle around the tree, not just at the base of the tree. Do this every week the first year of a tree's new life at your house, and do it once a month the second year. And be sure that the soil around your tree is moist at the end of the growing season, before the ground freezes.

Lawns: Water needs for lawns vary according to soil type, grass type, and age of the lawn, among other things. A new lawn needs pampering while its roots develop. A well-established lawn shouldn't need watering except in times of drought. It is better to water deeply once a week than a little every day. One inch per week is generally accepted as adequate.

Factors That Affect Water Needs

Type of plant: Each species of plant has a specific need for water. Cacti are renowned for going months without water. Cattails grow in swamps. Most plants are somewhere in between—they need that elusive "moist, well-drained soil" that garden books cite as best for everything from delphiniums to maple trees.

Soil type: Soils differ tremendously in the amount of moisture they can retain. Sandy soils retain very little, while clay soils hold on to water so strongly that they often stay too wet. A good silt-based loam will retain water but allow excess to drain off.

If you have sandy soil, you have three choices: a) grow plants with minimal water requirements, b) improve the soil by adding compost and organic matter to retain more water, or c) water like crazy. Clearly, the second option makes the most sense in the long run. Adding compost will improve wet clay soils by allowing excess water to drain and air to circulate, thus drying out the soil.

Slope: The slope of your garden matters, too. Imagine a parking lot on a hill. Turn on the hose. The water will run off quickly. Your soil acts the same way, even though you can't see it happening. Water in the ground is pulled downhill by gravity—unless it is captured and retained by soil particles or organic matter.

Sun and shade: The amount of sunshine your garden gets affects how much water it needs. A shady garden needs less water than a full-sun garden. Afternoon sun is stronger than morning sun and has more drying power.

Watering Techniques

Some gardeners prefer to water by hand with a hose (or even a watering can), supervising exactly how much each plant receives. Others like to turn on a sprinkler and forget about watering. There are devices to do your watering for you while you lie in the hammock with the *New York Times*—or this book. Here are some of your options.

Timers

If you are busy and are likely to forget about your plants, or if you'll be away for two weeks in August, buy a timer.

There are electronic timers and mechanical timers. If you have trouble getting rid of the blinking numbers on your VCR or microwave, buy a mechanical one. Timers can be set for a week's watering. You can have it water for an hour every day, or two hours every other day, or only—or never—on Sunday. They attach to the faucet where you attach your hose, and even the mechanical ones take a battery to run the clock. Buy the simplest timer you can. I once had one that could only be operated by nuclear physicists or MacArthur Fellows, and it didn't get much use.

Sprinklers

The simplest sprinklers are those that have no moving parts. These often look like a little brass animal (rabbit, toad, etc.) with a nozzle that sends out a fine mist up in a circle. The rate of flow and size of the circle depends on the water pressure you establish when you turn on the faucet.

Then there are simple spinning sprinklers. Three arms rotate around a central pivot, sending water quite a distance in a circle.

A reciprocating sprinkler or "flip-flopper" has an arm 18 inches long with lots of little holes that send out a fine mist. Water pressure moves the arm, spraying a rectangle of lawn or garden. This type of sprinkler can be adjusted to spray a larger or smaller area.

Rainbirds are the Cadillacs of sprinklers. Rainbird is actually a brand name, but the term is used for all of them, just as the word "Kleenex" is used generically. A metal tripod 6 feet tall supports a rotating nozzle that can spray water long distances. Again, there are ways of controlling just what is sprayed and what is not.

If you use an overhead sprinkler, measure its output by placing tin cans in various locations to determine how long it takes to deliver 1 inch of water.

Soaker Hoses

Soaker hoses are hoses that leak. No, not like the one your puppy chewed on. These are designed to leak—or ooze, really. They come in rolls, some that you cut to length, others all set to go. They need to be pinned down with 6-inch landscape staples to hold them in place, and then most gardeners cover them with mulch. Because soaker hoses release water slowly, they water only a very small area, an area just 1 or 2 feet wide the length of the hose. Installing them is labor intensive. A good soaking can take up to eight hours.

Soaker hoses can be used anywhere but most commonly appear in perennial gardens, where they are more or less permanently installed, wending their way around the flowers and shrubs. They can be used in vegetable gardens, but they usually need to be taken up and reinstalled every year to allow for tilling and planting.

The gardener at the Saint-Gaudens National Historic Site in Cornish uses soaker hoses—but without a layer of mulch. That way he can see when one breaks or malfunctions. The plantings are so close together that the plants hide the hoses.

Drip Irrigation Systems

Farmers and gardeners in California are masters at installing drip irrigation systems. Every garden center in California has all the parts you need to design and install a customized system. Here in New Hampshire parts are harder to find, but you can get parts through catalogs if you wish. Gardeners Supply Company sells complete kits with everything you need to set up a small drip irrigation system. Sprinkler Warehouse will sell you the components to design and build your own system of any size. See chapter 12 for their contact information.

Basically, a drip system consists of 1-inch plastic pipe that can be punctured with a little tool to install small-diameter hoses and emitters that deliver water exactly where you want it. Emitters deliver water at a specified rate in gallons per hour. If you run a pipe past a tree that needs lots of water, you can attach a section of ¼-inch hose to the pipe with several emitters, thus distributing the water exactly where you want it.

Watering Wands

Watering wands are wonderful. They attach to the end of your hose and consist of an aluminum pipe with a watering rosette on the end that delivers a nice gentle spray. They have a bend near the end of the pipe to make the angle of watering comfortable, and a plastic grip insulates the pipe so cold water doesn't chill your hands.

I don't like watering every inch of the garden, walkways and weeds included. Since I have good soil and well-mulched beds, I prefer to water just the plants that are newly planted or that seem to need a drink of water. My watering wand allows me to walk down a row of tomatoes, for example, pulling the hose behind me, stopping to water each tomato plant but nothing else. By adjusting the water pressure with a valve on the watering wand, I can deliver water gently or send out a lot.

Watering Cans

Every gardener should have a watering can. No need to buy a fancy metal one; plastic ones work just fine. They are the best way to water delicate seedlings that have just germinated, although a watering wand can be almost as gentle. Sometimes it's just less work to fill a watering can than to drag a hose over to a thirsty plant.

What Can You Do to Conserve Water? Mulch!

Mulching is the easiest and best way to conserve water. A hard rain on bare soil is likely to run off, not only missing the chance to give your plants moisture but also removing some precious topsoil. Mulch helps to prevent runoff and to retain water that has penetrated the soil. Mulch also helps to keep down weeds that might otherwise compete with your plants for water.

Straw, mulch hay, or leaves: In the vegetable garden my partner, Karen, and I use straw, mulch hay, or leaves. We let the soil warm up and dry out in the spring, then we put down a layer of newspapers (about six sheets thick) in the walkways and around our plants. We cover the newspaper with 3 to 4 inches of mulch. We find that our earthworms love newspapers, so most of the paper is decomposed by the end of the summer—adding more organic matter to the soil.

In the old days newspaper inks had toxic heavy metals that could accumulate in soils and be absorbed by plants. That is no longer the case. Inks today are soy based, even the colored inks. Unless your fingers get black from handling the paper, the newspaper was printed with soy ink and is safe to use around vegetables. If you are mulching the garden on a windy day, take the hose and wet down the papers before you try to spread them. Just run the hose into whatever type of bin you use to store the papers.

Leaves are the best mulch as far as I am concerned—both in the vegetable garden and the flower beds. I visited garden designer and writer Sydney Eddison in her garden during a major drought several years ago and was amazed at her soil: It

Will Mulching with Bark Chips Steal Nitrogen from My Plants?

No, I don't believe so, though it is often *said* that it will. The theory is, and this is true, that the soil microorganisms that break down bark chips need nitrogen from the soil to build proteins as they multiply. But I've never seen any ill effects. Nitrogen-starved plants have yellow leaves, and as much as I've used bark chips, I've never had a problem. If you are worried, top-dress with a slow-release organic fertilizer before you mulch. I always add some organic fertilizer and compost at planting time, which may be why I've never had a problem.

was moist, fluffy, and full of earthworms. Her secret? Mulching with leaves for thirty years or so. She uses leaves that have been run over by the lawn mower, which chops them into small pieces that decompose more quickly. She spreads the chopped leaves in the spring after all her perennials are up.

I rarely have enough leaves, but I save all I can. If your neighbors put theirs by the side of the road in bags for the town to collect, go get them! One word of warning: Ask your neighbors if they use pesticides of any kind on their lawn. If they used the lawn mower to suck up the leaves, you'll be getting grass, too, and you might be getting more than you bargained for: herbicides. I won't accept grass clippings from lawns that have been treated with "Weed-n-Feed" products.

Black plastic is used by some vegetable gardeners to control weeds and retain moisture. I don't like it because it looks ugly, creates water pockets for mosquitoes to breed in, and may negatively affect my soil microorganisms. I can't tell if the beneficial worms, bacteria, and fungi can survive and thrive in the soil under it, so I avoid it. I've tried it—it's an easy way to keep down weeds for large expanses of pumpkin patch—but I no longer use it.

Landscape fabric is a woven synthetic material that comes in rolls. This is best used under some of the mulches listed below. Water and air can pass through the fabric, but weeds cannot. The heavier types block out light, but the lighter ones do not. You need to buy special landscape staples to hold it in place. Landscape fabric is not ideal on steep hillsides, as mulch tends to slide off it and go downhill.

Landscape fabric can be effective for keeping out weeds but is labor intensive to install if you are cutting and fitting it around existing plants. New installations are easier: You cover your bed and then cut holes for plants. Some years later, as perennials or shrubs reach maturity, you may have to go back and cut away more fabric to allow plants to expand.

Bark chips: Every garden center sells a variety of bark chips—

some dark brown, others tan, others bright red; some coarse, some fine. Chips are primarily used in flower beds and around trees, places that don't get tilled every year. Many garden centers also sell bark chips in bulk, which is usually much cheaper. I prefer fine chips as they spread more easily, look more natural, and break down into usable organic matter faster.

If you buy chips in bags, read the labels. Avoid any that have been colored with dyes (as some of the red ones are), and watch out for those made from ground lumber. Some less-expensive types are made by chipping wooden pallets or construction debris.

Cocoa mulch is very fine, nice looking, and smells like chocolate chip cookies for a week or two. I've found that it will often turn moldy in the heat of the summer, though that disappears after a while. It can be slippery when wet and tends to slide downhill in the rain. I've used it but don't like it. It's also expensive, and I've heard that it can be poisonous to dogs silly enough to eat it.

Pebbles or river stone: Lovely to look at, smooth round pebbles can effectively hold in moisture and repress weeds. But if there are lots of weed seeds in the soil, weeds will pop up in between the pebbles. You can get around that by putting landscape fabric beneath the stone.

Knowing When to Water

How can you tell when it's time to water? Sink your fingers into the soil. Yes, there are moisture meters, but you don't need one. Soil should be lightly moist. Dig down 6 inches or more from time to time to see if moisture has penetrated deeply to where roots are.

Buy a rain gauge to see how much rain fell during the night or while you were at work. Remember, most plants do fine with an inch of rain per week. If you haven't gotten any rain in a week, check the soil to see if plants need watering. If you are using an overhead sprinkler of some kind, set out some empty jars to catch water and learn how much water is being applied per hour.

Distribute the jars around the area being watered, because many systems don't distribute an equal amount of water in each part of the spray pattern.

Watch for signs of stress. A good gardener can see plants starting to stress long before the plants collapse. Don't wait until plants wilt! By then they are almost ready for a trip to the emergency room. A constant supply of moisture keeps plants growing. When they wilt, plants are already shutting down their metabolic processes.

In hot weather plants grow faster and lose more water to transpiration, the plant equivalent of sweating. A newly planted broccoli plant might not need watering on a gray cool day but will suffer without water if it's in full sun on a 90-degree day.

Final Thoughts

Put the right plant in the right place, and you shouldn't need to water much when plants are mature. My friend Doris LeVarn of Meriden, an excellent gardener, rarely waters her south-facing flower bed, even in dry times. She has selected deep-rooted and drought-tolerant plants like sedums and grasses that can withstand drought without suffering.

The bottom line is, only water when the soil is very dry or if your plants start to look stressed. Don't overwater. Soil nutrients can wash away with too much rain or too much watering. A good soil will hold moisture and keep a reserve for your plants, so work on improving your soil. And if you use a sprinkler, run through it on a hot day. Sprinklers are not just for plants—or kids.

Green Things

CHAPTER FOUR

Vegetable Gardening

If I make it to heaven, I know there will be homegrown tomatoes there. And asparagus all year-round, and different colors of lettuce, peppers, and potatoes. But to hedge my bets, I grow all these things—even if I can't have them year-round. My family's vegetable garden is my pride and joy.

Some gardeners hesitate to grow vegetables because they think it is too much work given New Hampshire's short growing seasons. Or because their parents made them pull weeds for punishment when they were teenagers. But don't be daunted. Vegetable gardens are worth every moment you spend on them, and they need not take too much of your time.

Starting a Vegetable Patch from Scratch

A vegetable garden will be with you for many years, so do a little planning before sinking spade into soil. Think about how much work you are willing to take on. Select a good site and prepare the soil properly so the garden will be a success.

Determine How Much Vegetable Garden You Need

Start small. There is nothing more discouraging than digging up the lawn to create a huge garden, only to find out that your first efforts are not as successful as you dreamed. Gardening is a learning experience, so you shouldn't expect to have a perfect garden the first year. And it takes time to build a good soil that will produce a good crop.

An 8-by-12-foot garden is a good start. This will give you room for two wide beds, 30 inches each, with a walkway down the middle and a little buffer zone between the garden and the lawn. One row could be for growing six tomato plants, with some room left for a few potatoes; the other would have space for carrots, beets, lettuce, and other favorites. Of course, you can plant just one tomato if you prefer, and set up a fence for climbing beans or early peas, or plant zucchinis and cukes instead of tomatoes. It's your garden and you can plant whatever you want.

Determine How Much Sun You Need

The more sun, the better. To grow leafy things like lettuce, you can make do with four to six hours per day. For tomatoes and pumpkins and peppers, eight hours or more is best. What if you can get only six hours of sun? Go for it. You'll still get tomatoes, just not as many.

Situate your garden away from tall trees—and not just because they will shade your garden. Their roots extend farther than you can imagine, and the fine roots that you might not even notice will be sucking up water and nutrients. Imagine a wine glass on a dinner plate. The glass is the tree, the dinner plate the roots.

Lay Out the Garden

I am not a neatnik, but I find symmetry pleasing—as do most people. It doesn't take much work to set up your garden so that it is neat and attractive. Get some twine, a carpenter's framing square, a tape measure, and a handful of large nails or stakes. If you plan a rectangular garden, set the long sides going east–west so that tall plants like tomatoes won't shade out smaller things.

Tie the twine on a nail, push the nail in the ground, and stretch out the twine the length you have chosen, then push in another nail. Pull the string tight and tie it onto the second nail. Lay the framing square on the ground to establish a right angle before repeating the process for the short end (the end perpendicular to the first). And so on. If the angles are all 90 degrees, the diagonals will be equal in length.

Of course, if you prefer, you can lay out your garden in the shape of a half moon or a hexagon or a five-pointed star. Gardens should be pleasing in the eye of the beholder.

Remove the Sod

Do not, I repeat, *do not*, rent a rototiller and just chew up a section of lawn. That won't get rid of the grass, that will just aggravate it, and the grass roots will get back at you for years. You must remove the grass or it will keep regrowing from the roots you've chopped up.

Removing sod is laborious, but less so if you have the proper tools. Do a little every day until it's done instead of working out at the gym, perhaps. There is a motorized device called a sod lifter that you might be able to rent if you are planning a 25-by-50-foot garden, but for small ventures you can do it by hand.

Buy or borrow an edging tool. This tool has a sharp crescent-shaped blade on a long handle. When you step on the edger, it slices through the sod to just the right depth. Cut the sod into squares or rectangles with the edging tool, tipping the handle back and forth to loosen the grass chumps. Pull up the sod with a garden fork or rake, or roll it up with your hands. Save the sod for your (soon to be started) compost pile, or use it to patch bare spots elsewhere in the lawn.

Improve the Soil

Get your soil tested before you do much to find out the characteristics of your new garden's soil and what amendments it needs. See chapter 1 for details about soil tests and where to get then done.

If your new garden has been a lawn, it will probably be low in organic matter and fertility. I'm not a big fan of rototillers, but for a new garden they make sense—once you've removed the sod, that is. They will loosen up the soil and allow you to mix in compost or aged manure. Rent, or if you're lucky, borrow one. In my opinion, it's not worth buying a tiller.

Start by rototilling a new garden twice, once right after the other. A metal depth guide on the machine allows it to stay near the surface or to go deep. If the soil is hard packed, start shallow. Then till again, going as deep as you can. Loosening the soil down to a foot deep is good if you can. Only rototill when the soil is dry—or at least not soggy. (See chapter 1 for a test that will let you know if your soil is dry enough to rototill.) Preparing a new garden bed in the fall is a good way to get a jump on gardening in the spring.

Next you will need to add organic matter and minerals. The best thing you can add to your garden is good compost, but if you can't get enough, buy aged manure from a dairy farmer. Why not use fresh manure? Cows aren't efficient in processing the grass they eat, so viable seeds often pass right through them, meaning their fresh manure can introduce grass and weed seeds to your garden. Therefore, ask for the stuff that is two to three years old or that has been "hot composted." Some farmers turn their piles of barn scrapings with a front-end loader to aerate them and get them "working" and hot—fermenting fast enough to heat up and kill the weed seeds. Manure is ready to use when there are earthworms in it.

Four to 6 inches of compost or aged manure mixed into your soil will greatly improve it. Ask if the farmer will deliver right to your garden, and then arrange a day when the soil and grass are dry so the truck won't get stuck. Spread out the compost and work it into the top 6 inches of soil, either by hand (with a garden fork) or with a rototiller.

Add fertilizer when you are ready to plant, rather than when you rototill. That way the nutrients will not be dispersed into the garden walkways or down deeper than roots usually go.

There are two exceptions: Add rock or colloidal phosphate and limestone or wood ashes before you rototill. Rock phosphate is slow to become available to plants, and it does not normally migrate through the soil the way most amendments will. Limestone and wood ashes are inexpensive and best distributed everywhere.

Vegetable gardens need some minerals replenished every year to ensure maximum veggie production, and new gardens generally need more help than established ones.

Instead of the traditional chemical fertilizers, I recommend organic bagged fertilizers for two main reasons: First, they are slow release, which means the ingredients won't wash away the way chemical fertilizers will. Second, organic fertilizers provide trace minerals and other needed nutrients that are not present in chemical fertilizers.

Warning: Don't get sticker shock! Organic fertilizers cost twice as much as chemical fertilizers, but they are worth it. A fifty-pound bag should last you more than one season, so the cost is not so much on a per-year basis.

As explained in chapter 1, greensand and rock powders are also good soil amendments. I add these when I plant, stirring them in with bagged fertilizer where plants will be going.

Raise the Beds

After rototilling use a short-tined garden rake, shovel, or hoe to create raised beds that are mounded higher than the walkways. Beds should be 24 to 36 inches wide and 4 to 6 inches above the walkways—or higher. I recommend leaving the same raised beds in place year after year, merely adding compost or aged manure on top and working it into the top few inches.

Why raised beds? For starters, they reduce the chance that you, or your kids and dogs, will step on plants or the soil near plants. Your pathways are clearly defined with raised beds, even when plants are young. Traditional narrow rows of carrots or lettuce assume the roots are all very close to the plants, but plant biologists now know that roots spread far and wide. The fine roots of veggies are so small you can't see them. Stepping on soil compacts it, making it less hospitable to roots, and can cause root damage.

Raised beds also allow you to grow more plants per square foot than traditional beds. Imagine a single row of carrots, a path, another row of carrots (or beets, or whatever), another path, and so forth. Wide beds allow you to avoid having so many paths, hence more room for veggies.

Plant the Garden

Spacing seeds properly when planting will save you work later when it's time to thin out the extra plants. Small seeds are difficult to manipulate, so some gardeners pour them into one hand, then pinch and sprinkle them with the other. Some gardeners tear off a corner of the seed pack and try to pour them out slowly. Some buy devices that will hold seeds and allow you to trickle them out slowly. None of those methods are perfect.

My method is slow, but pretty easy. I wouldn't want to use it to sow a 50-foot bed of carrots, but for small quantities it's ideal. Here's what I do: I buy a ¼-inch wood dowel, cut off a 6-inch section, and sharpen it like a pencil. I place seeds in a bowl, then wet the tip of the dowel. When I touch a seed, the dowel picks it up like a magnet. When I touch the seed to the soil surface, it is released. You need to rewet the dowel, so bring along a bowl of water. This technique easily allows me to plant carrots an inch apart. It's great for planting things in six-packs, too.

Planting depth is listed on the side of the seed packet, but as a rule tiny seeds should be right on the surface and big seeds in holes three times as deep as the seed is long. I'd rather be closer to the surface than too deep. For tiny seeds sprinkle some fine soil, vermiculite, or soil-starting mix over the seeds. I do this by filling a kitchen colander with soil and shaking it over the seeds. Then I press down lightly with my hands, firming up the soil to get good contact between the soil and the seed.

Seed Choices: Heirloom versus Hybrid

In recent years gardeners in New Hampshire and elsewhere have been buying more and more heirloom seeds. These are seeds of

To Start Indoors or in the Ground?

Due to New Hampshire's short growing season, some plants must be started indoors or purchased as seedlings at a greenhouse that has done the work for you.

Here's a list of those that *should* be started early and when to start them: artichokes (2/15), brussels sprouts (3/1), broccoli (3/15), cabbage (3/15), cauliflower (4/1), eggplants (4/1), leeks (3/1), melons (4/1), onions by seed (3/1), peppers (3/1), tomatoes (4/1), and watermelons (4/1).

Others can be planted indoors to get a head start, including asparagus from seed (it's usually planted by root), beets (3/15, though rarely done) cucumbers (4/15), kale (3/15), lettuces (3/15), melons and pumpkins of all kinds (4/1), spinach (3/1), squashes of all kinds (4/1), and Swiss chard (3/15). These also can be sowed directly outdoors later.

Everything else? Plant seed directly in the ground. Read the seed packets for timing.

varieties that your grandparents—or even *their* grandparents—might have grown. Heirloom plants are not bred for transporting long distances or for fitting into standard cardboard boxes, so commercial growers tend to avoid them.

The 'Brandywine' tomato may be the best-known heirloom of the lot. It is a big, awkward-looking, slow-to-produce pinkish tomato that is also the best-tasting tomato I've ever tried.

Hybrid plants are the result of carefully pollinating one variety with another to get new varieties that have the best qualities of each parent. In particular, hybrids are grown for disease resistance, size, looks, and transportability. And many of them are excellent plants. Don't save seeds from hybrids—they won't breed true, and you probably wouldn't like what you got. You may wish to try some heirlooms and some hybrids, too.

Open-pollinated plants are those that are *not* hybrids. You can save seed from these plants, but some—such as those in the squash family—are a bit promiscuous and need to be kept away from their cousins if you plan to save seeds. If not, you'll get hybrids that might not be very tasty when you grow the seeds next year.

What about seeds from genetically modified organisms? Genetically modified organisms are much in the news these days. GMOs are made when scientists insert genes from one species into another, nonrelated species to confer resistance to herbicides or to produce built-in biological insecticides. Corn, soy, and other field crops have been developed as GMOs, but as far as I know, GMOs are not being sold to the home gardener and may never be. The cost of developing GMOs is very high, so seeds for home gardeners might never be produced.

Starting Seedlings Indoors

When I was young and too busy to mess around with seedlings in early spring, I bought seedlings at the local greenhouse. Later, lured by luscious color catalogs that offered varieties of tomatoes and

peppers that I couldn't find as seedlings, I started growing my own. Now it is one of my joys in life: starting unusual things indoors when winter feels like it will go on forever. I recommend it. Again, start small—one flat or two. I now start 300 seedlings or more each year, but I've had lots of practice.

What do you need? Lights. Buy a 4-foot, two-tube fluorescent shop light. A table in a cool room, preferably by a window. Temperatures 65 degrees during the day and cooling to 55 degrees at night are ideal. Plastic six-packs for individual seedlings and plastic flats (trays) to contain them. Be sure the flats are the kind that hold water (some have slits for drainage). Sterile potting or starting mix. Optional: a heat mat designed to be placed under a flat to warm seeds and speed germination. Enthusiasm.

Hang the lights over the table, about 6 inches above your seedlings. Hang the lights from something that will allow you to raise them as the plants grow. I hang mine from the ceiling, but I also have a plant stand with adjustable shelves. If you use the ceiling, get toggle bolts to hold the weight, as screws will eventually come out of drywall, wreaking havoc below. I use jack chain (a metal chain available at hardware stores) to hang the lights.

Some people start a few plants on the windowsill. What they get, however, are usually tall, spindly plants that are struggling. If you try windowsill gardening, keep the plants as close to the glass as possible, as the sun's strength dissipates quickly as you move the plants back from the window. The bottom line? New Hampshire's sun in the spring really isn't strong enough to do the job. Get some lights.

Six-packs for planting come in various sizes, from thirty-six cells per flat to ninety-six. I always go for bigger cells to allow more room for roots to grow and to keep the cells from drying out so quickly.

The standard way of starting seedlings is to use sterile mix, which is a peat-moss-based planting medium. Fill the six-packs with mix and add water. The mix will be very dry and probably resist getting wet; fill the flat partway with water and let the mix suck it up from below. That might take an hour or more.

Make a small divot in the planting mix with the tip of a pencil or a sharpened dowel and drop in a seed. I actually make two divots and add two seeds to ensure that at least one germinates.

Few Words about Seed Companies

I joke that the seed companies have spy satellites to see who needs their catalogs. Once you're on one list, it seems that you're on everybody's list. I like ordering seeds from New England companies like Johnny's Selected Seeds of Winslow, Maine, and High Mowing Seeds of Wolcott, Vermont. High Mowing is all organic and carries many heirloom varieties. Fedco Seeds of Maine is a cooperative, and its prices are low. Baker Creek Heirloom Seeds is a good source for old varieties. The Cook's Garden and Renee's Garden Seeds both have some wonderful varieties I can't find elsewhere. You'll find these companies listed in chapter 12.

To get good contact with the mix, press down lightly on it with your fingers. For tiny seeds I don't make a divot but place the seeds on the surface and sprinkle a fine layer of vermiculite on top. Vermiculite is heat-expanded mica sold as fine powder to hold water in sterile planting mixes.

It's critical that your seeds *not* dry out while they are waiting to germinate or when the seedlings are very young. The best way to prevent desiccation is to cover the flat with a clear plastic cover. These are sold along with the flats and, unlike the six-packs, can be reused each year. Some folks use Saran wrap or even a plate of glass to keep in moisture, but if some seeds germinate and send up tall seedlings while others are still snoozing, you have a problem. The clear covers will let the early birds get a couple of inches tall while waiting for late starters.

You can use anything for starting seeds: old margarine containers, yogurt cups, etc. Some gardeners like peat pots, but I do not: They tend to dry out faster than plastic. Others make pots of used newspapers wrapped around a form—too much work for me.

After germination, I take scissors and cut off the smaller of the two seedlings. The sooner you do this, the better. If they get too big, they're competing with each other and both suffer—and you'll be tempted to keep both.

Soil Blocks: Another Way of Starting Seedlings

If you're tired of buying sterile potting mix and those little plastic six-packs every year, there is an alternative: soil blocks. These are 2-inch cubes of soil, compost, and minerals made with a simple metal press available from seed companies like Fedco and Johnny's Selected Seeds. In recent years I've been using this technique, and I like it.

Most gardening books warn against using real soil when starting seeds because they say fungi in the soil could cause a disease called damping-off. Damping-off makes seedlings literally keel over and die, and there is little one can do to stop it. Using sterile mix minimizes the chances of that happening.

There is another way of looking at the situation, one that I prefer. I believe that using soil and compost introduces *beneficial* soil organisms in your planting blocks, helping plants to be healthy and resist disease. If you have good air circulation, adequate light, and a growing medium rich in nutrients, you should have plants that will succeed, not succumb. I've never lost seedlings to damping-off when using soil blocks.

Here's what I do: Using a two-quart juice pitcher, I measure out ten quarts of dry peat moss, put it in a wheelbarrow, and mix it with one quarter cup of limestone (to counteract the acidity of peat). Then I add ten quarts of coarse sand, ten quarts of peat humus (available in bags at garden centers), and one-half cup each of the following: colloidal phosphate (or rock phosphate), greensand, organic blood meal, and rock dust or Azomite (optional). I mix well, then add eight quarts of compost and eight quarts of rich garden soil. This recipe makes enough for about 500 blocks, but you can make a smaller batch—or share with your friends. The sheer messiness of this might make a good school project!

For a start I mix four quarts of the dry ingredients with one quart of water in a small plastic tub, stirring it with my hand (wearing a rubber glove). I add more water until the mix is gooey but firm, not watery.

To make blocks I make a pile of the gooey stuff 4 to 5 inches deep, then compress it by pushing down on it with the block maker. When the mix fills up the four cavities of the blocker, I get rid of any excess by pushing the blocker down against the bottom of the tub and rotating it.

The tool ejects the blocks with the squeeze of a spring-equipped handle. You can drop them right into a plastic flat, which is just the right width for the block maker. One flat holds eight rows—for a total of thirty-two blocks. Later you can water the blocks by adding water to the flat and letting the blocks suck it up.

The great thing about making soil blocks is this: Roots stop when they come to free air, so the young plants don't get root bound the way seedlings do in six-packs. At planting time the block goes into the soil, and the roots are not disturbed. A 12-inch tomato plant in a plastic cell of a six-pack has severely tangled roots that need to be teased out at planting time, which causes delays in growth until it recovers. The same size tomato plant grown in a block has roots ready to expand immediately.

Hardening Off Seedlings

You wouldn't fly to Miami in February and spend a day at the beach without hat or sunscreen. Nor should you take the seedlings that you've pampered indoors for eight weeks and suddenly put them outdoors in full sun and wind. Plants need hardening off, a process to get them toughened up to the sun and wind.

Start by carrying your seedlings outdoors and putting them in a place sheltered from the wind and where they can get a few hours of morning sun. The north side of the house is generally good for that. Bring them inside before the afternoon sun reaches them. Do that for a couple of days, then give them some afternoon sun, but water first if they are at all dry. Finally, let them have a sleepover, staying out all night. Be sure to bring them in if the temperature is going to get close to 32 degrees. I take an entire week to harden off my plants—but I may be an overly protective parent.

When to plant those hardened-off seedlings? A cloudy or drizzly day is best. Late after-

Ask at the Greenhouse: Is It Ready to Plant?

Very important: When you buy plants, ask if they have been hardened off. If not, your new purchases may get sunburned or set back in their growth if you put them right outside. Buying nonhardened-off plants may mean waiting to put the newcomers into the ground, even though *you* are ready to plant them.

noon or evening is better than morning, as your plants have time to settle in before exposure to a hot sun.

Planting Tips by Vegetable

Asparagus: Buy three-year-old roots if you can find them and plant them 4 to 6 inches deep. Add rock phosphate and organic fertilizer to the soil, plus lots of compost. Water regularly the first year for best success.

Beans: Buy some rhizobial bacterial powder before you plant. This will inoculate the plants with nitrogen-fixing bacteria, which will improve your soil. Moisten the seeds and sprinkle the powder on them. The same procedure goes for peas. And pick beans regularly to keep them coming.

Broccoli: Plant early and late: Start some seeds indoors and plant seedlings in late May; plant seeds in the ground in late June for a fall harvest. Don't plant when the soil is cold and wet—that will encourage cabbage maggots. The same goes for cabbage and others in the brassica family. Row covers are good for keeping off pests that affect broccoli and cabbage, such as flea beetles and cabbage worms.

Corn: Don't buy supersweet varieties; New Hampshire soil is too cold at planting time. If you crowd your corn, you will get smaller ears.

Garlic: Plant cloves in October and cover with 12 inches of straw or mulch hay. Garlic will grow through the mulch in spring, but weeds won't. Harvest in early August.

Horseradish: A little goes a long way, and never goes away. Plant by root where you can contain it with a lawn mower, as it spreads.

Lettuce: Plant seeds every two to three weeks from May to September and you'll always have plenty.

Onions: Starting onions from seed early in March is better than growing them from sets (little bulbs) in May. There are more varieties of seeds to choose from, and plants started from seed are often more vigorous.

Parsley: Soak seeds in very hot water for an hour or more to help them germinate faster.

Peppers, eggplants: These guys like it *hot*. Grow them under row covers until they flower. Even then, eggplants don't need insect pollinators, so they can stay covered. Chunks of dark rock placed near them absorb heat, helping them to stay warm at night

Potatoes: Cut seed potatoes into chunks, each with an eye or sprout, and let the cut surfaces dry for a day or two before planting. I use a post hole digger to dig holes 6 to 8 inches deep for planting. The chunks of potatoes grow roots below and your potatoes above, so add compost and organic fertilizer in the hole and stir, then plant—cut side down. They need 6 inches of soil over them to grow lots of spuds. As the shoots grow, fill in the hole to increase production.

Spinach: This is a cold-weather crop, so plant it early or late. Most varieties bolt when it's hot.

Sweet potatoes: This is a hot-weather crop. New Hampshire gardeners can only grow them successfully under black plastic in rich soil and with some kind of in-ground watering like soaker hoses.

Tomatoes: It's common to have tomato plants that are tall and leggy when it's time to put them in the ground. You can turn all that extra height into roots by pinching off the side shoots and planting your seedling *sideways*. That's right, just keep the top cluster of leaves and plant the seedling in a trench, not a hole. Turn up the top so the leaves are just out of the ground—the stem is flexible and won't snap.

Thinning Seedlings in the Garden

Imagine if your mother had given birth not only to you but also to eleven other siblings all at the same time. Imagine what it would be like if you all had to live in the same house and survive on the same amount of food your parents bought every week when you were growing up. That's what some unlucky lettuce, abused beets, and cruelly crowded carrots go through every year. Some gardeners cannot bear to thin their seedlings or don't have the time—and shame on them!

Thinning plants is critical to success in the garden. Vegetables compete with each other for moisture and nutrients just the way they compete with weeds. Thin early in the season, as soon as you can get your fingers on the young seedlings. You can transplant the thinned seedlings if you wish and if you have space.

Scissors are great for thinning. Just snip off seedlings at ground level when they are young. It doesn't disturb the roots of developing plants the way pulling them out might.

Pooh's Picks for Vegetables in New Hampshire

Since 1973 Pooh Sprague and his wife, Anne, have been growing and selling vegetables and flowers on 40 to 50 acres at Edgewater Farm in Plainfield. They grow everything from A to Z (artichokes to zucchini). Here are some of the varieties Pooh recommends, with a few of my favorites indicated:

Beans, bush—'Xera'

Beans, pole—'Kwintus' (my pick; stays tender even when large and freezes well)

Beets—'Golden Beet', very large; 'Detroit Red'; 'Chioggia', a sweet striped beet (my pick)

Broccoli—'Marathon', 'Arcadia'

Brussels sprouts—'Oliver'

Cabbage—'Storage #4'

Carrots—'Mokum', 'Rumba', 'Bolero'

Cauliflower—'Snow Crown', 'Amazing'

Celery—not worth growing in New Hampshire

Corn—no supersweets for New Hampshire; 'Mystique' (mid-season), 'Seneca' (late)

Cucumbers—'Straight 8', 'Marketmore'

Kale—'Red Russian', 'Winter Borer'

Leeks—'Tadorna', 'King Richard'

Lettuce—'Wildfire Mix', 'Sun Devil' (iceberg)

Melons—'Early Queen', 'Athena'

Onions—'Red Burgemaster', 'Walla-Walla', 'Copra' (great keeper)

Peas—'Knight', 'Sugar Anne' (edible pod)

Peppers, sweet—'Yankee Bell', 'Ace' (it ripens early to red)

Potatoes—'Russian Banana', 'Careeb', 'Yukon Gold' (I like 'Red Pontiac' and 'All Blue')

Radishes—'Cherry Bell'

Radishes, fall—'Red Meat' (I love these; plant them August 1)

Rhubarb—'McDonalds', 'Tilden'

Spinach—'Melody', 'Unipak'

Summer squash—'Multipik'

Swiss chard—'Fordhook'

Tomatoes—'Jet Star' (early, disease resistant), 'Red Agate' (grape), 'Striped German' (heirloom), 'Cherokee Purple' (heirloom), 'Brandywine' (heirloom and the best tasting of all), 'Big Beef', 'Sun Gold' (cherry, one of my favorites, and very prolific)

Zucchini—'Raven', 'Romanesco'

Final Thoughts

There's a folk song I love with a refrain that runs through my head each June when I plant the garden: "There's only two things that money can't buy: true love and homegrown tomatoes." Homegrown tomatoes. Sigh. I just wish I could have them all year round. Maybe one day I will.

Annual Flowers

Trends in horticulture go through distinct phases. When I was growing up in the 1950s, most people grew annuals: flowers that bloom for a season, then die. Petunias, marigolds, and ageratum graced every yard and garden. Then perennials came along, taking over the world of flowers. Now as I travel around the Granite State, I see that annuals are making a major resurgence.

Good looks count for a lot, but annuals are becoming more popular up here in cold country because many new varieties have been developed that don't whimper on chilly days in spring or fall. Plants that, like the Energizer Bunny, keep on going and going. Perennial flowers may come back every year, but they bloom for just a few weeks. Annuals are workhorses, producing blooms all summer long if you give them what they need. And they are great in containers.

Starting Annuals by Seed

There are lots of wonderful annuals that you can start from seed—saving you money and enabling you to get varieties that a small, neighborhood farm stand might not have. And if you have the time and space, you can grow a hundred of one kind of flower to use in Cousin Jeanne-Marie's wedding.

It makes sense to start most annuals in the house eight to twelve weeks before the last frost date. Yes, you can get them to bloom eventually if you sow seeds directly into the soil, but blossoms won't show up in your garden much before Labor Day.

If you want to start annual flowers by seed, read the seed packets carefully to determine when to start them indoors. Return to chapter 4 and follow the directions for starting vegetable seedlings.

Selecting Good Seedlings

Don't feel guilty if you'd rather buy seedlings than start seeds. Not everybody wants to germinate annuals in the house and tend seedlings for two to three months. By Mother's Day greenhouses are chock-full of bodacious hanging planters, thousands of six-packs, and plenty of small pots with flowers ready to follow you home. But be forewarned: Bigger isn't better.

Many annual flowers in six-packs are already in bloom in garden centers by the time you are ready to buy them. Each cell in those six-packs has very limited soil, and big plants often have big root systems—roots that are so tangled up from growing in the small cell that they won't expand unless you tease them out with a finger or a tool. Even so, the root-tangled plant may just sit there for a while, recovering and doing nothing. That's not good for us, the New Hampshire gardeners, who have such a short season.

Educate yourself. If you plan to buy plants, talk to knowledgeable friends, read the gardening magazines, and make a list before you go to the greenhouse. Instead of buying what's in bloom, buy small plants of things that will be gorgeous later. A good book on annuals is *Annuals for Every Purpose* by Larry Hodgson. It has hundreds of color photos, and all its care suggestions are for organic methods. Seed catalogs can be great reference guides, too.

Where should you buy seedlings? A friend recently lamented to me that he'd bought all his seedlings the previous year at a Big

Box store, thinking he'd save some money. He did, but he was sorely disappointed when they didn't perform well. Then he put on a fake Alabama accent and explained the problem from the point of view of plants that had traveled to New Hampshire: "Ah ain't gonna do nothin' for you folks up heeya. Ah din't like the trip and it's too dang cold at night."

I strongly recommend that you buy your seedlings only from family-run garden centers, farm stands, or greenhouses or go to your local farmer's market. Local folks know what varieties do well in our climate and how to grow them.

Plants that have dried out en route from South Carolina, for example, may have suffered root tip dieback that you can't see, and that will hinder growth all summer long. Somebody who means well (but works the rest of the year in hardware) may overwater plants in the Big Box store until they develop root rot. Locally grown plants are almost always good.

Care and Feeding of Annuals

Fertilizers: Annuals vary a lot in how much nitrogen-rich fertilizer they need. Many new varieties do better with regular fertilization—often they've been bred for container growing and expect a dose of chemical fertilizer every two weeks. But you don't have to use chemical fertilizers. All I do is add compost and a slow-release organic fertilizer to the soil at planting time, and my annuals do fine. You can spray fish and seaweed fertilizer on your plants in midsummer if you feel they need a pick-me-up.

Annuals in containers are often given *foliar fertilizers.* These are water-soluble fertilizers that are sprayed on. I use a one-quart hand sprayer with a teaspoon of Neptune's Harvest fish and seaweed fertilizer mixed in with the water to give a little boost to plants in pots that are looking tired or neglected. It lets them know I love them—and provides a little extra nitrogen.

> ## Plants That Need to Be Deadheaded
>
> Bachelor buttons, gazanias, geraniums, marigolds, osteospermum, pansies of all types, pincushion flower, salvias, snapdragons, sunflowers, verbenas, zinnias, and most flowers used as cut flowers do best if you deadhead them.

Watering: Annuals have smaller root systems than perennials, so they need to be watered more often. Big annuals in small pots can barely make it through an August afternoon without a drink of water. Don't wait until your plants droop before you water them.

Pinching: Despite what you were told in kindergarten, pinching is good. When growing annuals from seed, pinch the growing tip off when plants are 3 to 4 inches tall. The stem will bush out with three to five new stems. Pinch those back a month later, and the plants will bush out even more.

Deadheading: If annual bachelor buttons have brains, they only have one thing on their minds: sex. They want to grow up and produce more bachelor buttons. Which makes sense: If they don't set seeds, their lineage will die out when the frost comes. Unlike perennials or trees, each annual gets only one chance to reproduce.

Your job, if you want annuals to bloom all summer, is to cut off the spent flower heads—deadhead them—as soon as they are bedraggled and before the plant thinks it has made enough seeds to start the next generation. That said, there are plenty of annuals that have been bred to keep on blooming even if you don't dead-head them. Ask at your local greenhouse.

Using Annuals

To fill in the garden: Many perennials take a year or more to reach full size, so new flower beds sometimes look pretty empty: a few perennials spread out on a sea of bark mulch.

Enter the annual. After planting your perennials, get some six-packs of annuals and pop them in the ground. Annuals are much less expensive than perennials and will get big fast and look good all summer long. You can buy a dozen annuals for the price of one perennial. But leave 8 to 12 inches between your annuals so they have room to grow without pushing and shoving each other.

In containers: Gardeners have been growing plants in pots at least since the times of Queen Hatshepsut of Thebes, Egypt, who reigned from 1504 to 1482 B.C. Ancient wall paintings show clay pots being used to transport trees that produced myrrh, a fragrant resin. The mutiny on the HMS *Bounty* occurred on a voyage carrying breadfruit trees in pots to the West Indies to start plantations producing cheap food to feed

How Much Root Space in a Pot Does Each Plant Need?

A 6-inch cube of soil is ideal. Many containers potted up by nurseries pack a lot of plants into a pot to make it look good so you'll buy it. But later, as the plants grow, they are too crowded. If you make up your own window boxes or pots, leave space for plants to grow. That way plants won't use up all the water so quickly in hot weather. Bigger plants need more space. Deep containers are the way to go.

slaves. And all our grandmothers grew red geraniums in pots or window boxes, I'd bet.

If you buy a hanging planter or fancy pot full of gorgeous blossoms, you must keep on fertilizing the container all summer long. Container plants need a light, fluffy growing medium so that air and water can get to roots, but they also need lots of nitrogen. The commercial potting mixes used for growing flowers in containers are fluffy but are mostly peat moss and perlite, which have little or no nutritional value. Your plants will need fertilizer added every two weeks.

Instead of fertilizing with a chemical fertilizer, you can use a liquid fish or fish and seaweed fertilizer such as those made by Neptune's Harvest. This will give your annuals micronutrients in addition to the N-P-K that your plants need. Or you can scratch a little Pro-Gro on the surface of the soil mix from time to time.

The Classics

Some gardeners turn up their noses at the best-known annuals because they've "been there, done that." Not me. There are good reasons why marigolds and zinnias are popular, and if you haven't grown them, you should. Many old favorites have new varieties you might not know about. Here are a few of my favorites.

Alyssum or sweet alyssum: A low-growing white, peach, pink, or purple flower loaded with hundreds of tiny blossoms. They start easily from seed, or you can buy six-packs. Plant them 8 inches apart. They will bloom all summer and into the fall, surviving some frosts. Their fragrance is said to repel deer and attract beneficial insects that eat aphids. None of the deer I've tried to interview, however, have been willing to comment—so alyssum's repellent qualities may be mythical.

Marigolds: Not only are they bright and cheery, they are thought to offer certain repellant qualities—to predatory bugs, not to you or me, but that may be just a tale. It *is* known that the roots exude

Latin Names

You will notice that some Latin plants names are used in this chapter and again in the chapters about perennials and trees. Don't worry about pronunciation: Every letter is pronounced, and even the experts don't agree on how to pronounce *Clematis*, for example. Common names can vary from state to state, but Latin names are precise—the same all over the world.

Latin names consist of two words. The first is the genus, which is like your family name, Jones, for example. All your relatives also have first names, but in Latin we put that second. Some Latin genus names are also the common name, such as *Delphinium*. The second name is called the species name; in general species don't interbreed. If they do, their progeny are called hybrids.

To make things even more confusing, "hybrid" is a term also used to describe plants created by crossing different varieties or cultivars of the same species. The words "cultivar" and "variety" are used pretty much interchangeably. The main thing to remember about hybrids is that they won't breed true, so don't save their seeds if you want the same type of plant next year.

If several species of a genus are described in writing, the genus name can be abbreviated as its first letter only. Thus *Lobelia cardinalis* is spelled out for a first mention, then *L. splendens* and *L. siphilitica* for its cousins. If you want to refer to all the species of *Lobelia*, you can write *Lobelia* spp.

A note for Rodney Dangerfield: If you learn a few Latin names, you'll immediately get some respect from serious gardeners.

a chemical that will kill nematodes, a type of worm that can eat the roots of plants (though plenty of other nematodes are benign). You can plant marigolds by seed after danger of frost or indoors a month before that. Average soil is fine; don't bother fertilizing.

Nasturtiums: Plant these sprawling beauties in ordinary or poor soil, as rich soil or added fertilizer will produce lots of leaves but few flowers. Idea: Plant nasturtiums over daffodils to hide the foliage. The seeds are large, so they are easy for kids to handle. All parts of nasturtiums are edible, and you can even pickle the buds or green seedpods and use them like capers. The spicy flowers are great in salads.

Petunias: Even though standard, old-fashioned petunias are getting elbowed out by newer hybrids, they are still good plants. They should be started indoors eight to ten weeks before last frost. The seeds are small, but some companies are selling pelletized seeds for ease of handling. Pelletized seeds are coated in a fine clay to make them bigger.

Snapdragons: These flowers are perfect for cold-weather climates: They don't need hot summers and will survive many frosts in the fall. Ask a child to watch when you squeeze on the sides of a blossom: The mouth opens just like a dragon's. Start seed indoors in April or buy seedlings. Cut off any flowers at planting time, and deadhead regularly. Picking flowers encourages bushiness, too.

Sunflowers: No longer just big, tall plants that produce bird food, sunflowers now come in many sizes and colors. They get their name from their obsession: the sun. Plant seeds outdoors after danger of frost. Most won't bloom until the late summer days get shorter, so buy *day-neutral* varieties if you want earlier results. Day-neutral varieties are not affected by day length.

The multiheaded varieties are the best bang for the buck, and they make great cut flowers. I love 'Teddy Bear' for its fuzzy yellow blossoms on 3- to 4-foot stems (and for the name), as well as all of the red/mahogany-petaled ones like 'Moulin Rouge' and 'Velvet Queen'. Get a seed catalog and drool over the sunflowers in February. Some are pollen free, which means they won't drop yellow pollen on your tablecloth.

Zinnias: Great cut flowers, these range in size from 3- or 4-foot giants (Benary's series) to 12-inch plants great for ground cover or containers (Profusion series) and everything in between. I love a lime green one called 'Envy' (as in green with . . .) or 'Benary's Giant Lime'—both are standouts as cut flowers. If you buy seedlings, get the smallest plants you can, as the bigger ones don't transplant well. And the more you pinch and cut the stems, the more flowers you get. There are some called 'Cut and Come Again' zinnias, which is precisely what they are!

Great Cut Flowers

If you want flowers in vases all over the house, plant a patch of flowers just for that purpose. Don't worry about garden design— just take over a part of the vegetable patch in full sun.

Greg Berger is the owner and flower guru at Spring Ledge Farm in New London. He started working there as a fifteen-year-old, went to college to study plants, and came right back. Since 1993 he has been running a cut flower business for Spring Ledge, and he recently bought the business. Here are some of his recommendations for varieties of annual cutting flowers that do well in New Hampshire.

Ageratum: 'Blue Horizon' (*Ageratum houstonianum*). Blue, long-lasting 3-inch clusters on long stems.

Brazilian verbena: (*Verbena bonariensis*). Purple blue small panicles of flowers on stiff wiry stems up to 48 inches tall. Somewhat frost tolerant.

Calendula: 'Kablouna Mix' (*Calendula officinalis*). Shades of orange and yellow. Eighteen to 24 inches.

China aster: 'Irresistible' Series (*Callistephus chinensis*). Pink, purple, and white, fully double 3-inch blooms with a three-week vase life. Very disease resistant.

Corn cockle: 'Ocean Pearls' (*Agrostema githago*). White 1- to 2-inch five-petaled blossoms on willowy gray stems.

Cosmos: 'Psyche Mix' (*Cosmos bipinnatus*). Red, white, and burgundy singles and doubles. Don't fertilize, otherwise they get too tall and don't flower as well. Forty-eight to 60 inches.

Flowering tobacco: 'Fragrant White' (*Nicotiana alata*). White. Scent is strongest in the evening. Forty-eight to 60 inches.

What's Hot in Annuals

Many of the newer varieties of annuals, the flowers every gardener is clamoring for, are patented. Best known are the Proven Winner series of flowers, which are genetic clones, propagated by taking cuttings and rooting them. Your local greenhouse will buy tiny plants—plugs—in the spring from wholesalers, pot them up, and tend them for eight weeks or more. Each one comes with a little tag saying "Proven Winner" that indicates it has come through the system properly and that no one is cheating by making unauthorized cuttings.

These new annuals are hybrids, the result of years of breeding. You probably won't be able to buy them in six-packs. They'll be in 4-inch pots and a bit pricier than you'd like, but worth every penny you pay. Most will do fine in cool weather, but don't expect them to stand up to frost, except for those marked "perennial," of which there are also plenty.

Among the popular Proven Winner annuals, Supertunia and Surfinia are petunia hybrids; Million Bells and Superbells are similar to petunias, but with smaller flowers and more blossoms per plant. Here are a few of the better-known varieties that do well in New Hampshire:

- Petunia hybrids—all the Supertunias and Surfinias
- Twinspur (*Diascia* hybrid)—'Flying Colors'
- Superbells (*Calibrachoa* hybrid)—'Cherry Red'
- Million bells (*Calibrachoa* hybrid)—'Cherry Pink'
- Nemesia—'Safari' Series

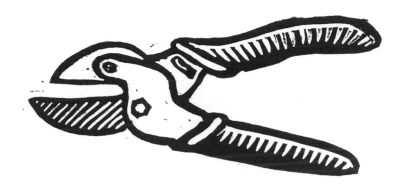

Larkspur: 'Blue Cloud' (*Consolida regalis*). Deep blue, looks like a delphinium. Small, delicate flowers. Seeds need cold to germinate; plant will self-sow. Thirty-six to 48 inches.

Pincushion flower: 'Giant Hybrid Mix' (*Scabiosa atropurpurea*). Mixed colors, including a violet so deep it's almost black. Sweetly fragrant. Twenty-four to 36 inches.

Salvia: 'Marble Arch Mix' (*Salvia viridis*). Rose and blue purple frost-tolerant blooms. Self sows. Twenty-six to 28 inches.

Salvia: 'Victoria' (*S. farinacea*). Deep blue blossoms on tall stems above handsome foliage. Drought resistant, likes poor soil. Twenty-four to 36 inches.

Snapdragons: 'Rocket Mix' (*Antirrhinum majus*). Yellows, reds, pinks, white on plants 18 to 24 inches tall. Somewhat frost hardy.

Zinnia: 'Benary's Giant Formula Mix' (*Zinnia elegans*). Mixed colors. Large blossoms on stiff stems hold up well to summer heat. Forty to 50 inches.

When and how do you pick cut flowers? Pick in the morning before it gets too hot or at dusk. Bring a plastic bucket or one of those tall, narrow metal picking buckets full of water. Plunging flower stems immediately into deep water prolongs the blossoms' vase life. Let them rest in the water for an hour or more if you have to pick them in the heat of the day.

Recut the stems when you make an arrangement, but remember the five-second rule: Lynn Schad of Bloemenwinkel Floral and Design Studio in Lebanon insists that no more than five seconds should elapse from the time you recut a flower to the time it goes in the vase.

Cut flowers will last longer if you change the water and recut the stems regularly. Mix up a gallon of "flower power" water by adding a tablespoon of sugar and a quarter of a teaspoon of bleach.

Tender Perennials Used as Annuals

If you've moved to New Hampshire from California or from below the Mason-Dixon Line, you know these plants—but you probably consider them perennials. Not here. These need to be dug up and brought inside or they will die come winter.

Bedding geraniums (*Pelargonium* x *hortum*): Chances are that your grandmother grew red geraniums. Mine did. You can start these from seed in mid-February or buy plants in May. 'Black Velvet' is an easy one to start from seed. I bring geraniums into the house each fall and keep them as houseplants. Cuttings taken in April will root in water.

Fuchsias: These come as both sun-loving and shade-loving varieties that are commonly used in planters. They are not generally started as seed. You can winter these over in a cool (50 degrees), dark basement. My gardening friend Doris LeVarn of Meriden cuts them back by half in the fall, then lets them dry out and go dormant. She brings them up and gives them a good dose of fertilizer six weeks before putting out. She uses the same procedure for Mexican sage (except no fertilizer) and *Brugmansia*.

Dahlias: Because of our short season, New Hampshire gardeners often get dahlia blossoms only in September. Many of the bigger varieties take 120 days to bloom, or even more. But there are early, mid-season, and late-season varieties. You can even start the small types from seed in February and get blossoms by midsummer. Harlequin Mix, 'Phantom', 'Figaro', and 'Opera' all work from seed. Buy tubers of 'Park Princess', 'Bonne Espirit', 'Red Cap', or 'Yvonne' for early blooms. If you want to grow dinner-plate dahlias, start tubers in pots inside and transplant outside in June.

At the end of the season, dig up tubers a week or two after frost and bring them inside. Pack the tubers in slightly moist sphagnum moss in paper bags and store at 50 degrees.

Foliage Plants

I grow some of my favorite annuals not for their flowers but for their leaves. These beauties are always *in bloom*—which is to say, their leaves are a treat to look at. I love their bright colors and shiny surfaces.

Perilla (*Perilla frutescens*): This is a terrific purple-leaf plant that self-sows exuberantly. Pinch off the flowers (which are not at all showy) if you don't want it to spread next year. It gets 18 inches tall. The 'Magellanica' hybrid has pink and green mixed in, too.

Persian shield (*Strobilanthes dyerianus*): This plant just shimmers with silver overtones on dark purple and pink leaves. It loves hot weather and gets big: One plant can spread over a 3-foot circle and stand 3 to 4 feet tall.

Sun-loving coleus: Long used as a colorful foliage plant for shady nooks, new strains developed in the 1990s do well in full sun. Colors range from deep crimson to brilliant chartreuse and golden sunset orange. Some plants have three or more colors on a single leaf. They like rich, moist soil and need to be 2 feet apart if planted in the ground.

Licorice plant (*Helichrysum petiolare*): I buy some of this every summer because I love the silvery leaves, because it mixes so well with bright colored flowers in planters, and because it takes abuse. It rarely complains if I let it dry out in a pot. It flows over the edges of pots and weaves its way through other plants. It's an exceptional accent in flower arrangements. There are also lime green and chartreuse cultivars.

Elephant ear (*Colocasia esculenta*): The huge leaves of this tropical plant look indeed like elephant ears. It comes in green or purple, and it loves wet locations. Plant elephant ears in full sun in a swampy area and it will delight you. It's expensive, so dig up the tuber in the fall and store in a cool dry place.

Vines

Annual vines are great for growing through climbing roses and on archways and trellises. Here are three good ones.

Scarlet runner bean: Red orange flowers and edible beans grow on this vine that will climb 15 feet or more in a single season.

Purple hyacinth bean (*Lablab purpureus* or *Dolichos lablab*): The glossy dark leaves and pink purple flowers of this fast-growing vine are edible, not just the beans. Very striking.

Morning glory: It's best to start these directly in the soil as they don't like being transplanted. Soak seeds overnight in warm water. Hummingbirds love the blossoms. Grows in full sun and average soil.

Annuals for Shade

Shady corners need more than green ground covers to come alive. Here are some bright, easy flowers for shade.

Impatiens is the best-known flowering shade plant and a surefire favorite because it will bloom continuously all summer with little care. You will need to buy plants, as it is not easy to start from seed, but you can make more plants by taking cuttings and rooting them in water. Impatiens likes rich, moist soil and will grow in full shade to part sun.

Begonias: There are two types, wax begonias (*Begonias semperflorens*) and tuberous begonias (*B. tuberhybrida*). Wax begonias have masses of small flowers and waxy green leaves. Tuberous begonias have much more dramatic blossoms—larger, with peaches, reds, and bicolors readily available. Neither is easy to start from seed. Tuberous begonias need to go dormant in winter, so dig up the tubers and store them like dahlia tubers. Wax begonias in pots make nice houseplants for the winter.

Browallia: This beauty comes in violet and purple, contrasting nicely with impatiens. It needs rich, moist soil and suffers badly if you plant it in a pot and don't water it regularly. It has 1- to 2-inch trumpet-shaped flowers, and hybrids are available with either cascading or bushy habits.

Edging lobelia (*Lobelia erinus*): Annual lobelia is sold everywhere in six-packs and most commonly has small intense blue or purple flowers. It will grow in full sun to full shade, but it tends to go dormant in midsummer. Fix that by cutting it back by one-half as soon as it starts to look ratty, and it will rebloom until frost. Don't let it dry out!

Lesser-Known Greats

Not all great annual flowers are well known. Be the first on your block to try these three beauties.

Angelonia: A bit like a snapdragon, this comes in white, pink, dark purple, and blue. It likes heat, is drought tolerant, and allegedly is not interesting to deer.

Gaura: This is said to be a perennial in Zone 5 and warmer, but don't depend on it here in New Hampshire. It has wonderful pink, almost orchidlike flowers growing all along long stems that tend to sprawl. 'Siskiyou Pink' is a nice one.

Euphorbia 'Diamond Frost': Another great Proven Winner, this is the Energizer Bunny personified: It produces small white flowers *all* the time. It is an airy, open plant with small leaves and delicate flowers. It grows in full sun to part shade, reaching a foot tall and wide. Bring it in for the winter.

Final Thoughts

The day of the first hard frost in the fall is always a depressing one for me. The cosmos are black and falling over. The leaves of dahlias are turning to mush. Those tasty nasturtiums whose flowers have graced our salads have given up the ghost.

At that point some gardeners just walk away from the garden and call it a year. The smart ones clean up the garden and remove dead plants so that diseases and insect pests won't winter over. Me? I keep puttering in the garden until the snow flies. But by then my annuals are long gone—until next year.

CHAPTER SIX

Perennial Flowers and Bulbs

I love perennials. They connect me with the seasons, filling me with anticipation each year: Have they survived our New Hampshire winter? Most do. They send up leaves, then flower stalks. They bloom and fade away. Some bloom early; others wait until after fall frosts. Every week from March until Thanksgiving, I cut flowers and put them on the table—even here in New Hampshire, with its short season and unpredictable weather. All that thanks to our perennials and bulb plants.

I've grown hundreds of different kinds of perennials (defined as flowers that come back every year but die to the ground each fall.) Some perennials die out after a few years, but others will outlive me. I transplanted a peony that was first planted in 1954 at my childhood home in Connecticut, and it's still blooming for me here.

I'm including some lesser-known bulb plants in this chapter because they extend our season of flowers greatly. Between 1995 and 2005 I picked fresh flowers—snowdrops—outdoors on March 4 every year but one. And in 2006 our snowdrops were budded up before Valentine's Day. Quite amazing. Colchicum and some true fall crocuses bloom for me late into the fall, sometimes to Thanksgiving.

What Do Perennials Need?

The needs of perennials are as different as the shapes of snowflakes. In nature they found their own little niches and excelled there before we tamed them and introduced them to our gardens. There are *at least* five factors that are important in getting a perennial to perform well and come back every year: amount of sun, type of soil, pH of the soil, amount of moisture held in the soil, and lowest temperatures of winter.

There are some limits, of course. You *can* grow a desert plant in New Hampshire, you just can't grow it in a bog. Sun lovers will survive in the shade, they just don't bloom as much or get so big. Even plants that would rather be living in Pennsylvania can be grown here—if the other four conditions for success are met.

Sun: Sun-loving perennials need six hours of direct sunshine per day for best results, and preferably more. But four hours of afternoon sun will suffice, or six hours of sun filtered through a sparse canopy of deciduous trees. Planting a sun lover in the dense shade of a hemlock or spruce tree isn't a good plan if you want it to bloom.

Morning sun is less powerful than afternoon sun. If you want to grow a shade lover in a sunny spot, plant it where it only gets morning sun. The same number of hours of afternoon sun might be fatal or at least cause its leaves to discolor. In general shade plants will do better in sunshine if they have consistently moist soil, not dry soil.

Soil type: You can adjust soil conditions to suit most plants. The vast majority of perennials want the same thing: rich, dark soil full of organic matter that stays lightly moist but not soggy. If your soil doesn't fit the bill, add compost or old manure—two or three shovels of compost worked into the area around the site for the new perennial. I add a cup of organic fertilizer and half a cup each of greensand, rock phosphate, and rock powder and stir it in well.

If you want a lean soil, meaning one without much nitrogen, don't add fertilizer. If a plant needs sandy soil, dig a hole and take

How Big a Hole Should I Dig?

When planting a perennial, don't just dig a hole the size of the pot. That's like buying snug sneakers for a teenager. For a perennial in a one-gallon pot (7 inches wide and 8 inches deep), loosen up and improve the soil in a 2-foot-diameter circle and about 1 foot deep. If you are planting something that will get huge, say a clump of phlox, prepare a wider hole. And for plants with deep roots like peonies, dig deeper.

away the soil in your wheelbarrow. Bring in sand and mix it with compost, two shovels of compost for every one of sand, then stir in some of the soil from the edges of the hole.

Soil pH: The vast majority of perennials like a slightly acidic soil, in the range of pH 6.0 to 6.8. Soil in the woods or fields of New Hampshire is naturally quite acidic; if you are planting in soil that has not been gardened in recent times, your soil will need to be sweetened—that is, made less acidic. Get it tested to see how much ground limestone to add when you plant your perennials.

If your soil test reveals a pH above 7.0, you can make your soil more acidic by adding elemental sulfur (approved for use by organic gardeners) or by using an organic fertilizer such as Pro-Holly or Holly-Tone. All of those soil additives take time—months—to change the pH. And follow the directions. More is not better.

Soil moisture: Adding compost and organic matter will improve soil's ability to process water. If you are planting a dozen perennials in a new flower bed, it doesn't make sense to improve the soil only in the holes where you intend to put each plant. Add a layer of compost 4 to 6 inches thick to the entire bed and work it in all over. That will *really* do something good for your soil: improving soil tilth and structure, helping your soil drain better in wet times, and holding water in hot, dry months.

How to Grow Moisture-Loving Plants on a Dry Hillside

A large plastic bag buried deep beneath a perennial will help retain water and can make a big difference in a plant's performance. I planted two moisture-loving plants, astilbes, side by side on a dry hillside; in each case I added compost and the minerals I normally use. But for one, I also "planted" a black plastic bag about a foot beneath the surface and poked a few holes in it with my pocketknife. The astilbe planted over the bag has become a much bigger, more impressive plant.

Soil temperature: You might not think you can do much about New Hampshire's cold winters, but you can. If you have a plant that is marginally hardy for your zone, wait until the ground freezes, then mulch it with wood chips or leaves. This will accomplish two things: It will minimize freezing and thawing, which can push plants up and expose their roots to air. And it will act as a blanket against extreme cold.

Fortunately most years we have a good, thick layer of snow on the ground for the coldest parts of winter, which acts as a blanket, protecting roots. Cold can travel sideways, too, so don't plant tender perennials near the edge of a terrace.

The Classics

Here is a generous baker's dozen of my favorite perennials. Every New Hampshire garden should have most of these, if not all. There are many other greats, but these are all easy to grow and most are hardy throughout New Hampshire—from the Canadian border to the Massachusetts line. A few are marked hardy only to Zone 4, but they would probably survive even in the coldest spots in the state if the soil conditions were right. These beauties are listed in the order they bloom in my garden.

Primroses (*Primula* spp.): There are many species of primroses, most of which bloom in spring or early summer. In general they like moist, rich soil in filtered shade or morning sun. They seem to love growing under big old apple trees. My favorite is a relatively unknown one with no common name, *P. kisoana*; it has pinky magenta blossoms, and for me it spreads fast by root in either moist or dry soil. Its fuzzy leaves make a great ground cover.

Another easy one is the drumstick primrose (*P. denticulata*). These bloom early with globelike clusters of purple, white, or lavender flowers on stems 8 inches tall. Another great one is the candelabra primrose (*P. japonica*), which blooms in June, displaying tiers of flowers on bare stems 18 to 24 inches above the leaves.

Bleeding heart (*Dicentra spectabilis*): Given rich, slightly moist soil and half a day of sun or more, this beauty will grow to 3 feet tall and wide in a few years. It has long sprays of small deep pink and white blossoms and blooms for three to four weeks. The leaves tend to yellow and die by mid-August in dry soils or hot sunny locations but they stay looking good later in moist soil or locations with morning sun only. They have deep fleshy taproots and do not transplant easily, but they often self-sow and the small seedlings move easily. Bleeding heart comes in a pure white form, *D. alba* ("alba" means white in Latin).

Peonies (*Paeonia* spp.): These are dramatic, wonderful flowers—many with scents so lovely as to nearly make one swoon. They are not without problems, however: Many of them have double flowers, meaning that they have many layers of petals, which makes them prone to flopping when wet. You need to stake these plants or buy peony cages to surround them. There are single varieties, with just one set of petals, and these rarely flop. My favorite double is 'Festiva Maxima', a fragrant double white with just a drop of red in the middle.

Peonies will live forever, almost, if planted well. They have deep taproots, so planting even a small one means digging a hole 2 feet deep and 2 feet across and filling it with rich soil, compost, minerals, and fertilizer. They need sweet soil, so mix a cup of ground limestone or two cups of wood ashes into the soil at planting time.

Siberian iris (*Iris siberica*): These bloom at about the same time as peonies, and the two make a wonderful combination. Iris blossoms are short lived but come in deep, rich blues and purples that are almost heart-stoppingly beautiful. They need to be divided every five years or so because they use up the soil nutrients and gradually the center of a clump dies out. Top-dressing early in spring with organic fertilizer (that is, sprinkling some fertilizer on top of the clump) helps to minimize this.

Delphinium (*Delphinium* spp.): These are spectacular flowers. Some of the bigger ones (Pacific hybrids, for example) send up flower stems 5 feet tall (or more) in rich blues and purples. But like peonies they must be staked, and even then they sometimes break in rainstorms. They need fertile soil in full sun. Ann Sprague of Edgewater Farm in Plainfield recommends a shorter variety known as 'Blue Butterfly', which is less than 2 feet tall, as one that rarely flops. *D. chinensis* is also short with delicate, fernlike foliage. To minimize flopping and encourage reblooming, cut stems right to the ground after blooming. Top-dress with organic fertilizer each spring.

Lilies (*Lilium* spp.): These beauties, both the Orientals and the Asiatics, are in trouble. The lily leaf beetle has devastated lilies in southern New Hampshire, and the beetles are moving north. So far I have been able to keep them under control by picking the red beetles daily. (See chapter 10 for more information combating these pests.) The Oriental lilies are fragrant, big, and brassy. The Asiatics are unscented and a little more delicate.

Daylilies (*Hemerocallis* spp.): Daylilies are indestructible and will grow just about anywhere. Dump a clump of roots on your lawn? Next year it will be a handsome plant. Not true lilies, they are

not affected by
the lily leaf beetle,
either. They prefer full
sun and good soil but will
grow anywhere.

There are fanatics out there
breeding and hybridizing daylilies,
so you'll find literally thousands of
named cultivars. The best-known is the
old-fashioned foundation lily, a bright
orange. But daylilies come in various pastels,
some with dark eyes, others with ruffled edges.
Some are early bloomers, some bloom late into the
fall; some flower *scapes* (leafless stems) are under 1
foot high, most are 18 to 30 inches, and a few reach 6
feet.

Perennial bachelor buttons (*Centaurea montana*):
Spidery blue 2-inch blossoms on 18-inch stems appear in early
summer, but if you cut them back—or pick the blossoms for
vases—the plants should rebloom for you at least once. They may
self-seed, appearing where you didn't plant them. It's a fairly
drought tolerant plant.

Foxglove (*Digitalis* spp.): The most common foxglove, *D. pur-
purea*, is not a perennial at all, even though it is often sold as such.
It's a biennial, a flower that gets established its first year of life, then
blooms, sets seed, and dies in its second year. The flower stems are

lined with small pink and purple blossoms that bloom on stalks from 18 to 36 inches tall. When the tiny seeds are black and ripe, cut a stem and shake it over an area where you'd like plants in two years. I do this along the edges of woods or fields. Foxgloves have so many seeds that a few grow even though I don't prepare the soil.

There is one cultivar, 'Foxy', that will bloom the first year if started indoors early, which is nice for Zone 3 gardeners, as foxglove is a Zone 4 plant. There are perennial foxgloves such as *D. lutea*, a smaller, delicate brown-freckled yellow, that is a perennial even in Zone 3.

Catmint (*Nepeta x faassenii*): Related to catnip, this is a hybrid plant with silvery gray mounding foliage and small trumpet-shaped blue flowers. 'Six Hills Giant' is one of the best cultivars. Cut catmint back after flowering and it will rebloom.

Pink mallow (*Malva alcea*): I know that "serious" gardeners, the ones who only use Latin names, will laugh at me for this choice and call it a thug. It's a generous plant: big, blowsy, pink, and beautiful; some might even call it slatternly. Plenty of blossoms, plenty of babies. I love it for its midsummer cheeriness. Not a great cut flower. It has a fleshy taproot and doesn't transplant well. Get a tiny one from a friend in early spring—we all have it. Deadhead it regularly to keep it blooming and to minimize volunteer seedlings; shear it back by a third in early June for smaller plant size.

Bee balm (*Monarda didyma*): Bee balm is big (3 to 4 feet) and beautiful, fragrant (minty), colorful (mainly in shades of red and purple), and a great cut flower. It likes full sun, but mine flourish with morning sun and good soil. It blooms in mid- to late summer, a time when many gardens need blooms.

Its flaw? It spreads by root and can quickly overwhelm a flower bed when you turn your back on it for ten minutes. Or a season or two. But it pulls up easily, so I don't consider it a thug. I've tried containing it with plastic edging, but still it wandered. It can get covered with unsightly mildew, but newer varieties have been bred to minimize that.

Shasta daisies (*Leucanthemum x superbum*): This white daisy is a great cut flower and a cheery addition to any garden. It is a short-lived perennial unless you divide it every two or three years, in which case it stays vigorous. It needs full sun and doesn't want to spend the winter in a soggy soil.

Sneezeweed (*Helenium autumnale*): This great fall flower has clusters of small daisy-family flowers on tall stems in interesting colors: mahogany and red and yellow, sometimes all three on each blossom. There's a pure yellow one, others with dark red as the dominant color. It likes full sun and tolerates moist soils. Hardy to Zone 4.

FYI: Sneezeweed is not a big allergy producer. I've read that it got its common name from the fact that back in days of taking snuff, it was sometimes ground and inhaled to stimulate sneezing.

Lesser-Known Perennials

Jill Nooney of Lee is an amazing gardener, garden designer, and sculptor of garden art who, with her husband, Bob Munger, has some of the most dazzling perennial gardens in the state. She opens them to the public four times a summer (see her Web site www.finegarden.com for dates). They are well worth a visit. Her property is Zone 5, so we can't all grow everything she does, but I'm willing to try some Zone 5 plants in my Zone 4 garden and hope for the best. Here are some unusual plants she loves.

Woodland peony (*Paeonia obovata*): Jill says she would grow this peony for the seeds, even if the blossoms were not part of the show. The blossoms, very simple singles in pink or white, produce seedpods in the fall that are stunning: They burst open with red berries and blue berries that stand out over the blue green leaves. It grows in part sun to light shade and may be hardy to Zone 4.

Threadleaf ironweed (*Vernonia lettermannii*): Most ironweeds are giants—4 to 7 feet tall with intense purple flowers in flat clusters at the top of their stems; in my experience they tend to flop unless staked. This one, according to Jill, is a native species sold by the New England Wild Flower Society (www.newfs.org) and is only 18 to 24 inches tall, a manageable size.

Maximilian sunflower (*Helianthus maximiliani*): This is a giant perennial sunflower 4 to 10 feet tall that produces clusters of 2- to 3-inch yellow flowers. Stems seldom need staking. It will grow in moist soil—or very dry soil. Zone 4.

Cardamine pratensis: Light pink to white flowers appear on this low-growing perennial in spring. It prefers part shade. Handsome rounded leaves. Zone 3.

Goldenstar (*Chrysogonum virginianum*): A ground cover with waxy green leaves and handsome yellow flowers in spring and fall. About 18 inches tall, it spreads and likes moist, well-drained soil in sun or shade. Zone 5.

Stonecrop 'Matrona' (*Sedum* hybrid): Pale pink upright flowers appear in late summer over gray-green leaves with rosy edges. Dark burgundy stems are a knockout. Jill suggests cutting this plant back twice, once in June, once in July, to keep it low, thus avoiding broken stems or flopping. She says it propagates easily: Just poke holes in the soil with your finger and stick the trimmings in for more plants. Zone 3. Readily available at nurseries.

My own picks for lesser-known perennials include two perennial lobelias. The first is cardinal flower (*Lobelia cardinalis*), which has fire-engine red flowers on 3-foot spikes, blooming in late summer in moist soil in full sun. Don't buy the fancy hybrids (peach, mauve, etc.). They don't overwinter well. Great blue lobelia (*L. siphilitica*) is similar to cardinal flower but shorter with intense blue purple flowers. It grows anywhere—and everywhere—and will compete with weeds. It has popped up a hundred yards from where I planted it. Too beautiful to be a thug, it pulls up easily.

Shade Perennials

Shade perennials, in general, are more understated than the flashy full-sun flowers. Primroses, a shade plant discussed in the "Classics" section, *are* dramatic, and astilbes can be, too.

Lungwort (*Pulmonaria* spp.): This is a very early bloomer with spotted leaves that look good all summer long. The small blossoms come in blue, red, white, and peach— and sometimes more than one color blossom on the same plant. Spreads by root.

Wild (or fringed) bleeding heart (*Dicentra exemia*): Sold in all nurseries, it isn't really wild anymore. It is one of the few perennials that will bloom most of the summer if soil stays moist. It has small pink to purple or white heart-shaped flowers.

Astilbe (*Astilbe* spp.): These do best with rich, moist soil; they also grow in sun if plenty of moisture is present. Bushy, airy flower spikes of tiny blossoms come in shades of red, pink, and white. They are excellent cut flowers with strong stems, so grow plenty.

European wild ginger (*Asarum europaeum*): This is grown for its glossy round 2- to 3-inch wide leaves. It likes rich soil and tolerates dry soil.

Hostas (*Hosta* spp.): Every garden center will have plenty of these, the backbone of shade gardens. Their leaves come in all sizes and colors from blue green to lime green and from tiny to huge.

Sweet woodruff (*Galium odoratum*): This lesser-known gem has leaves arranged in whorls around the stem and dainty white, fragrant flowers in June. It spreads nicely by root in moist soils; in dry soils the foliage may die out in August. An excellent ground cover.

Wildflowers

New Hampshire is rich in wildflowers, so I can't discuss them all here. But here are three great ones that are often available in garden centers. The New England Wild Flower Society (see chapter 12) also sells hundreds of kinds of wildflowers at the Garden in the Woods, in Framingham, Massachusetts. Go in spring for a real treat.

Please do not dig up wildflowers from the woods and bring them home. You'll most likely fail—most don't transplant well. And you may adversely affect their population in the woods.

Jack-in-the-pulpit (*Arisaema triphyllum*): Not only is the strange-looking flower (a dark figure—Jack—sheathed in a green curled leafy arrangement) interesting in spring, it shows off with red berries in the late summer. It does best in rich, moist soil and medium shade, though I also have it in dry soil—it's just not as vigorous. Zone 4.

Trillium (*Trillium* spp.): Another great genus of wildflowers everyone should grow. Trilliums have three leaves on a solitary stem and deep purple or white three-petaled flowers above the leaves. Trillium blooms in early spring and prefers moist, well-drained soils. Most species are hardy to Zone 3.

Bloodroot (*Sanguinaria canadensis*): Bloodroot's green leaves emerge very early in spring, rolled up like cigars, opening to round leaves 5 to 8 inches in diameter. The white flowers last just a few days, but they are true harbingers of spring for me. Doubles, though frightfully expensive, look like miniature white roses, and they bloom longer than the singles. Leaves stay nice all summer if the plant is grown in slightly moist light shade. Zone 3.

Lesser-Known Bulb Plants

Everyone knows the standard flowering bulbs: crocuses, daffodils, hyacinths, and tulips. They're great plants, but there are also bulb plants that are equally good but not so common.

Most bulbs need well-drained soil. Early spring bloomers can be planted under deciduous trees—the bulbs get their sunshine to charge them up for another season before the tree leaves shade them. Here are some of my favorites (all are hardy to Zone 3 unless otherwise noted).

Snowdrops (*Galanthus nivalis*): These guys must have kerosene in their veins, as they are undaunted by cold and literally push up through frozen soil every year. Their tiny white blossoms are best shown off in large numbers, so start with fifty bulbs if you can. Divide after blooming every few years; they multiply nicely.

Winter aconite (*Eranthis hyemalis*): Bright yellow, these are almost as early as snowdrops. They have buttercup-like flowers that hug the ground. Hardy to Zone 4.

Scilla (*Scilla siberica*): These small, intensely purple flowers are early bloomers, following and overlapping with snowdrops. Many are needed for a good show.

Glory-of-the-snow (*Chionodoxa luciliae*): These are also early bloomers, appearing with scilla. They have vivid blue flowers with light-colored centers. I like these better than scilla because they look up, showing their faces, while scilla look downward.

Grape hyacinth (*Muscari* spp.): These cuties look vaguely like a 2-inch cluster of grapes upside down on a 3-inch stem. They bloom mid-spring and come in a variety of blues, purples, whites, and bicolors. Unlike most other bulbs, they send up a few leaves in the fall. I use them as markers—I plant some with my daffodils or tulips to mark locations where I shouldn't dig when planting bulbs in the fall.

Allium **spp.:** These are wonderful relatives of the onions and chives you already know. My favorites include the drumstick allium (*A. sphaerocephalo*n), which has 1- to 2-inch clusters of reddish purple blossoms at the tips of thin, wiry stems 18 to 24 inches long. Great cut flowers, and, if dried, will look good for a year in an arrangement.

Then there is *A. giganteum* (hardy to Zone 4), which has a stem 3 to 4 feet tall with a globe of florets 5 to 6 inches in diameter. Truly spectacular. The seedpods look good long after the bloom. Star-of-Persia (*A. christophii*) has even bigger blossoms, reminiscent of fireworks. Both are hardy to Zone 4.

If you grow leeks in the vegetable garden, let a few winter over: They will bloom magnificently their second year, though then you can't eat the leek. All alliums are wonderful.

Colchicum (*Colchicum autumnale*): These gems look like crocuses on steroids. The bulbs are large and should be planted in late summer or early fall. They come as singles or doubles and in pinky-lavender or white. They surprise me every fall as they pop out of the ground without the accompaniment of leaves. The leaves appear in spring, then disappear.

Each bulb may send up half a dozen blossoms in sequence; their only failing is that they flop. Plant a ground cover like sweet woodruff or vinca around colchicums to help prop them up. They bloom very late in the season. I also use them as cut flowers.

Fall crocus (*Crocus sativus, C. speciosus*): These crocuses are very late, sometimes blooming until Thanksgiving, and often producing more than one blossom per bulb. Less hardy than spring crocuses, some will die off in hard winters in Zone 4, but all should be good for Zone 5. Plant in fall for fall bloom.

Final Thoughts

Growing perennials can become an obsession. There have been times when I couldn't visit a garden center without filling up my vehicle with plants. Now I've pretty much run out of space in the garden, so I show more restraint. But the beauty of perennial flowers still stuns me, and I'm in love every day with another one—whatever is in bloom. So watch out.

Trees and Shrubs

In 1970 when I bought the house I live in today, I didn't know much about gardening. Sure, I could grow vegetables, and I knew some flowers I liked. I could identify the trees that grew in the woods—I'd been a Boy Scout, after all. But I didn't give much thought to planting trees. And shrubs? We had evergreen muffin-shaped things growing in front of my boyhood home, but I had little interest in them—or other shrubs. I wish I had.

If I were to buy a house today, I'd start right away planting trees and shrubs. These "woodies" take the longest to reach maturity, yet they can truly transform a landscape. Blossoms, foliage, bark, silhouette: Trees and shrubs have something to offer New Hampshire gardeners year-round. Trees and shrubs provide structure to the landscape, forms that don't disappear in our long winters. They can be used to create outdoor rooms and special places to relax in privacy. They are often referred to as the bones of a garden, around which the meat of the garden grows.

How to Plant Trees

Planting a tree involves much more than just digging a big hole and plunking in a sapling. Planted too deeply, most trees will never make it to maturity or will limp along and never reach their potential. Bark—resistant to rot above ground—will rot underground. A deeply planted tree will slowly decline until, by age ten or fifteen, it is ready for the woodpile. Here's the proper way to plant any tree.

First, Find the Trunk Flare

Your mission, before you dig a hole, is to find the trunk flare of your young tree and then make sure it's above ground once planted. Look at trees growing in the forest. Notice how the trunk flares out and "roots" appear to snake across the ground a little before disappearing beneath the surface. That flare must be above ground to grow a healthy tree.

Commercial growers plant trees like corn, close together in rows. When the trees reach a certain size the trees are pulled up (without soil); some are slapped into a pot right away, others are shipped first. In either case, the pot is filled with soil and nobody worries much about trunk flare.

Take a good look at the tree you're about to plant. Can you see the trunk flare? If not, you need to remove soil from the surface until you find it. Take your time. The flare may be covered by 3 to 6 inches of soil in the pot, depending on the size of the pot.

Small fibrous roots may have started growing above the trunk flare if it's been buried in soil for a year or more at the nursery. Ignore or trim off those rootlets. Keep looking for the point at which the trunk flares out. It is not always easy, especially for very small trees.

Digging the Hole

Having found the trunk flair, measure the distance from it to the bottom of the pot. That's how deep your hole should be, no deeper. That means your tree will be sitting on unexcavated soil—so it won't settle later—and the flare will be visible.

It's always better to plant a tree in a hole that is a little shallow rather than in a hole that is too deep. For large trees, some experts prefer to feel around for the trunk flare, but they don't remove all the soil covering it at planting time. Instead, they advise you to let it get settled in for a year, then remove the excess soil that is covering the trunk flare the second year. But don't forget to do this!

A planting hole should have gently sloping sides and be three to four times as wide as the root-ball. Why so wide? Even after you backfill the hole, the soil will be looser than the soil in surrounding areas, allowing fine roots to penetrate it more easily.

Normally you shouldn't add compost or fertilizer to the soil when you backfill the hole. You don't want to create a bathtub of good soil that encourages roots to stay put, enjoying a life of luxury, as it were. You want them to extend far and wide, and they will have to get used to whatever native soil you have.

In cases of extremely poor soil, dig a much wider hole and mix the crummy soil half and half with good garden soil—even if you have to buy it. But be sure to choose a tree that can survive in poor soils if that's what you have.

What can you do to help the tree get established? Sprinkle a one-pound coffee can full of rock or colloidal phosphate in the bottom of the hole, and scratch in. Mix in another can of the same into the backfill. Rock phosphate doesn't move through soil easily, and it promotes good root growth. Azomite or rock powders are good to add, too.

Planting

As you backfill the hole, carefully pack the soil around the root-ball with your hands or tamp it with the handle of your spade. You want to eliminate any air pockets. After filling the hole half way, water the soil well. Go have a cup of coffee and come back after the water has soaked in, then finish filling the hole.

Create a raised lip of soil at the edge of your planting to hold in water. That way water won't run off and will soak down deep. Water once or twice a week. A sprinkler mimics rain, which is good; put out a tuna can to see how long it takes the sprinkler to deliver an inch of rain, the amount you should provide with each watering. If using a sprinkler isn't practical, use a bucket and provide five gallons each time. Young trees need some watering their second year, too, particularly if New Hampshire has a hot, dry summer.

Cover the planting zone with 2 to 3 inches of bark mulch, but keep the mulch away from the trunk. You don't want to cover the trunk flare with mulch, as it will cause bark rot. Mulch volcanoes, though common, can be deadly.

Before I knew better, I planted an apple tree in a deep hole full of manure and garden soil. I covered the trunk flare. The roots stayed in the bathtub I'd created. The trunk rotted. I never got more than a couple of apples from that tree, and I yanked it out after ten years. Don't make my mistakes!

Taking Care of the Newly Planted Tree

Once planted, trees really need very little care. Mother Nature doesn't supply fertilizer spikes or spray pesticides, and you don't need to, either. There are two things you can do that will vastly improve the chances of a newly planted tree surviving: Water it regularly, and protect it from weed whackers (string trimmers). To keep the weed

When to Plant a Tree

There are two schools of thought on this. I prefer planting trees in the fall, as it's cooler and generally we have more rain. Roots continue to grow even after leaf drop, and without leaves to lose moisture there is less chance of dehydration—a major cause of death in young trees.

The other school of thought is that our winters are harsh, so we should let trees get established all summer before they face the cold. This requires that you water your new tree once a week all summer long. Don't keep the soil saturated, but don't let it dry out. If you can do that, planting in spring is fine.

whackers away from your tree, mulch around it so there will be no grass or weeds nearby, or plant a ground cover that need not be mowed. If the bark gets sliced through by a string trimmer or lawn mower, nutrients and water are cut off from a portion of the tree. If the tree is girdled, it will die. No second chance.

Pruning Deciduous Trees and Shrubs

Most people look forward to pruning their trees and shrubs about as much as they look forward to going to the dentist. As a result, many planted trees and (especially) shrubs are formless, messy, and cluttered. I love to prune. It is an opportunity to create sculpture, but without the tedious chipping away of granite or wood with a chisel. I think most people don't prune because they don't know just what to do, and they are afraid of doing something awful, something irreversible to their precious tree or shrub. Better to leave it till next year than make a mistake now, many think. The trouble is that "next year" never comes.

March is the best time to prune fruit trees. Evergreens should be pruned in early summer, just after they have put on their new growth. Fall is a good time to prune deciduous trees and shrubs (those that that lose their leaves). Once they have lost their leaves, it is easy to see their form—and their problems. Insects and diseases are dormant and less likely to attack an open wound in fall.

A word or two first about tools to use: The technology has changed in the past twenty years, so you should think about getting some new tools. Sharp is important. That rusty old-fashioned bow saw you've had hanging in the garage for years is *not* what you want.

Pruning saws now have tricut blades with teeth so sharp that they go through hardwood like the proverbial hot knife through butter. This is good: A sharp saw gives a clean cut and doesn't tear. The new saws can't be sharpened, or not by most of us, but they are worth the price and will last for years if you keep them clean and don't misuse them by cutting roots. Bypass pruning shears and loppers are also needed.

Before you begin pruning, it is important to know where to make your cuts. Although trees vary considerably in the shape of their branches, most have a swollen area called the branch collar where the branch meets the trunk or a larger branch. Often you will see wrinkled bark at the outer edge of the branch collar. It is important not to cut into the collar but to prune just beyond it.

The collar produces chemicals against invading disease. A flush cut tight to the trunk removes this important area and opens up a large area to disease. In the 1950s we were told to make flush cuts and to paint them with tar. Now research indicates that these are not good practices.

If you are cutting a large branch, you need to make three cuts to remove the branch without risk of tearing the bark and damaging the collar. Remove most of the weight of the branch by making two quick cuts: First, make an undercut about one-third of the way through the branch to be removed—about 12 inches from the branch collar. This will prevent a tear from extending into the collar. Then, a little farther out the branch (away from the trunk), make a top cut that will sever the branch. Finally make a cut at the edge of the branch collar, removing the stub that you just created. Since the stub is lightweight, there is little danger of tearing.

Now you are ready for surgery. Stand back and look at the tree or shrub. Is the form pleasing to you? Do you see strong lines? Is it the shape you hoped for when you bought it? Keep these thoughts in mind as you get to work.

The first step is to remove all deadwood. This might seem tricky in fall without leaves to guide you, but it isn't. Dead branches are brittle, their color is different, and their bark may be flaking off. If you scrape the bark on a branch with your fingernail, a live branch will show green; a dead branch will not. You can remove deadwood anytime of the year.

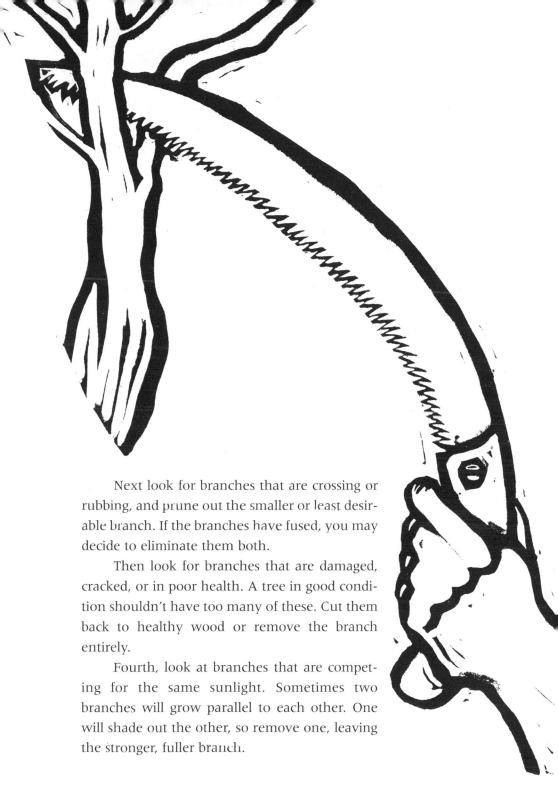

Next look for branches that are crossing or rubbing, and prune out the smaller or least desirable branch. If the branches have fused, you may decide to eliminate them both.

Then look for branches that are damaged, cracked, or in poor health. A tree in good condition shouldn't have too many of these. Cut them back to healthy wood or remove the branch entirely.

Fourth, look at branches that are competing for the same sunlight. Sometimes two branches will grow parallel to each other. One will shade out the other, so remove one, leaving the stronger, fuller branch.

Fifth, eliminate the "invaders." These are branches that spot an opportunity to catch some sunlight and reach out for it like a teenager going for the last cookie on the plate. Invaders ignore the basic branching patterns and clutter up the interior of your tree or shrub. Often they become rubbing or crossing branches.

Lastly, prune out water sprouts. These are small branches that tend to shoot straight up from larger branches. They are often a response to a tree in stress, a tree's way of producing extra leaves and thus additional capacity to make food.

Many fruit trees produce numerous water sprouts every year. In the heat of the summer the leaves at the top of the tree become dormant due to the heat. The interior part of the tree is cooler and remains better able to produce food. Instead of eliminating all of the water sprouts, try training a few to fill in the interior of the tree. This should slow down the annual production of water sprouts.

For years I followed the pruning rule that it was all right to remove up to one-third of a tree each year if necessary. Current thinking is that it is better to remove only 15 to 20 percent of the live branches on any given year. Cutting off branches may make your tree look better, but you are also reducing its ability to produce food. So take out all the deadwood, but be moderate in eliminating healthy branches.

Some shrubs, such as lilac and forsythia, will withstand severe pruning without suffering. When thinning multistemmed shrubs, cut back the oldest branches all the way to the ground. This allows younger, more vigorous stems to predominate.

Pruning can make a scruffy shrub a thing of beauty. Don't be afraid to try your hand at it; almost anything you do is fixable. Trees and shrubs will respond to pruning by becoming healthier and more vigorous. If you take off a branch in an "oops!" moment, another will eventually take its place. Take your time, especially at first, and step back often to look at the entire plant. You will be rewarded not only with a more handsome plant but also a better appreciation for its form, texture, and personality.

Pruning Evergreens

Pruning evergreens is done largely to keep trees and shrubs from getting too big. Blue spruces, for example, are sometimes purchased when small and cute. People are shocked to find them blocking their windows and reaching skyward just a few years later.

Pines, spruce, and hemlocks don't get cluttered up with water sprouts or invaders: Their branches grow in nice neat rows off the main trunk.

To keep an evergreen small, prune off each year's new growth when you can still see the difference in color between new and old growth. Generally that is in June. It is very difficult to keep a tree small if it is programmed to be 60 feet. If you want a small evergreen, get a dwarf cultivar, or one that grows very, very slowly.

Good Trees for New Hampshire

New Hampshire is home to dozens of species of wonderful native trees. You probably know the sugar maple, white birch, white pine, and Canadian hemlock. But many other species of trees are hardy here, including some uncommon ones that you may wish to see and eventually to plant.

Steve Sweedler is the horticulturist at Plymouth State University in Plymouth. He has been planting trees at the college for about three decades and has turned the campus into one of the best informal arboretums I have ever seen. Plymouth is a Zone 4 area, but Sweedler grows many Zone 5 trees in protected places. Here are five of his favorite trees.

Yellowwood (*Cladrastis kentukea*). Zone 4, full sun. Growth rate: medium. Size: 30 to 50 feet tall and wide. A native of the southeastern United States, "it will stop traffic when it blooms," says Sweedler. The pealike, fragrant white blossoms hang down in 6- to 9-inch terminal panicles in May or June. Yellowwood tends to put on a great show every second or third year. The bark is gray and

smooth. Fall foliage is yellow.

Paperbark maple (*Acer griseum*). Zone 5, full sun. Growth rate: slow. Size: Eventually it can reach 20 feet high and perhaps 15 wide. The best part of this tree is the color of its exfoliating (shedding) bark: It has variegated rich reds, browns, and cinnamon colors. The trunk is "muscular and smooth, a knockout," according to Sweedler.

Dr. Merrill magnolia (*Magnolia* x *loebneri* 'Merrill'). Zone 4 or colder, full sun. Growth rate: fast. Size: 25 to 30 feet tall and wide. Like Sweedler, I love the blossoms—white and 3 inches or more across and fragrant—that appear in late April before the leaves emerge. The flower buds are large and furry all winter, which is nice. Great glossy dark green foliage all summer, good enough to use in flower arrangements. Handsome gray bark.

Japanese umbrella pine (*Sciadopitys verticillata*). Zone 5, full sun to light shade. Growth rate: very slow. Size: 20 to 30 feet tall by 15 or 20 feet wide. The leaves (needles 2 to 5 inches long) radiate around the stem in whorls and are extremely dark green, almost black at times. Sweedler has one specimen growing in front of a brick building, and he loves it best in winter when the contrast against the snow is outstanding.

Katsura tree (*Cercidiphyllum japonicum*). Zone 4, full sun. Growth rate: medium to fast. Size: 40 to 60 feet tall by 20 to 30 feet. National tree expert Michael Dirr, author of my tree bible, *Manual of Woody Landscape Plants*, describes this tree this way. "If I could use only one tree this would be my first tree." Sweedler puts it high on his list, too, for the bluish cast to its foliage and for its overall beauty. Bark gets shaggy as the tree gets older.

Shrubs

Shrubs are really just trees that never get big. Most grow as multi-stemmed plants, sending up several stalks from the ground. They are much more forgiving than trees when it comes to covering the trunk flare—and for some, trunk flare is not noticeable. But follow the same procedure for planting shrubs as you do for trees.

The Classics

New Hampshire gardeners have favored a handful of shrubs over the years, so much so that some gardeners consider them trite and tend to avoid them. I disagree. They are classics: handsome year-round, undaunted by our winters, and willing to grow almost any-where.

Lilacs (*Syringa* spp): Zone 3. The common lilac (*S. vulgaris*) may have been named the New Hampshire state flower for its lovely, fragrant flowers that, for many, are symbols of early summer and invoke memories of the "good old days." Or perhaps because they grow everywhere in the state.

Lilacs prefer full sun but will survive anywhere. They flower most profusely in soil that is neutral, so people have been spreading wood ashes over their roots each spring for centuries. It doesn't really matter when you spread the ashes, and you can use limestone if you don't have a woodstove. Three or four coffee cans of wood ashes (or two to three cans of limestone) distributed around the base of a mature lilac each year is plenty.

Lilacs can live for a hundred years or more but get less vigorous and produce fewer flowers as they age. Prevent this by thinning out the older canes (stems) every few years, cutting them right to the ground. Many of the older varieties send up root suckers—unwanted shoots popping up nearby. Unless you prune suckers out every year, your lilac will spread, becoming a cluttered mess.

There are many species of lilacs and more than 800 named cultivars. By buying several you can extend the season of blooms to six weeks. 'Miss Kim' is a nice Manchurian lilac (*S. patula*) developed at the University of New Hampshire that grows slowly, stays small, and blooms after the common lilacs. The Japanese tree lilac (*S. reticulata*) is a small tree form that blooms in July—but may fill your woods with seedlings. Some consider it invasive.

Hydrangeas: Zone 3. With their white snowball flowers in the late summer, these shrubs are popular everywhere, from farmhouse to cemetery. The "peegee" hydrangea is the best known. Its common name derives from the Latin: *Hydrangea paniculata grandiflora*. It grows fast, even in poor soil, and blooms when other shrubs are not blooming. Hard to kill. Pick the blossoms in the fall before frost and save in a dry vase for winter arrangements. The *H. tardiva* blooms later and has conical blossom panicles.

Forsythia: Zone 4, though blossoms can be killed by hard winters. One of the first shrubs to bloom in the spring, forsythia is known for its dazzling yellow flowers and for the fact that a few plants spaced 5 feet apart will quickly become a dense hedge. I like it best pruned to a vase-shaped shrub, but root suckers will fill in around your original plant if you don't prune them out. 'New Hampshire Gold', 'Vermont Sun', and 'Northern Sun' are cultivars that do well in our climate.

Only in the last few decades have there been forsythia that would bloom reliably every spring. Paul Joly of Cornish crossed two forsythia and created the New Hampshire Gold hybrid in 1966. It bloomed from top to bottom, no matter how cold the winter. Like hydrangeas, forsythia will grow anywhere and you can't kill them.

Roses: Zones 3 to 5 or 6, depending on variety. It's true that long-stemmed English tea roses can be finicky and are best grown as annuals in the colder parts of the state, but there are plenty of good roses are that are fully hardy. The Canadian Explorer series of roses, developed in Ottawa, are hybrid roses that have rugosa roses in their parentage and were bred for hardiness and disease resistance. Rugosa roses, also known as beach roses, are nearly indestructible but have smaller blossoms and short stems. They do have large hips, or seedpods, that can be decorative all winter. I love *Rosa glauca*, a rose with a purplish hue to its leaves.

Mike Lowe of Lowe's Roses in Nashua (www.loweroses.com) grows a thousand different types of roses. He suggests planting a rose in a hole 2 feet deep by 3 feet wide and filling it with a 50-50 mix of sandy loam and compost. He suggests buying bare root roses and planting them in the early spring.

Lowe gave me several tricks he swears by: In the bottom of the planting hole, put a 3-inch square of gypsum wallboard and two or three large nails. He also noted that roses grafted onto root stock should be planted so the graft scar is *below* the soil surface. Lastly, he told me that roses *love* water. Water them regularly, even in rainy summers, and they will perform well for you. Five gallons a week per rose is good.

Azaleas and rhododendrons: These shrubs will grow in part shade or full sun, producing colorful blossoms and shiny green leaves. They like acidic soil and have shallow, fibrous roots; most don't do well if the roots are constantly wet. If you have a heavy clay soil, amend it with peat moss and compost at planting time, and plant the azalea or rhodie in a mound that is a little higher than the surrounding soil.

The PJM rhododendrons are bright and colorful and tough as nails. The original PJM is a purple pink, but others now come in a variety of colors, including white. They bloom reliably year after year in Zone 4 or warmer. Steve Sweedler likes *R. mucronulatum* 'Cornell Pink' because it blooms so early.

When it comes to cold hardiness, it's hard to beat the Northern Lights azaleas. They are hardy and will bloom after winter temperatures of 40 degrees below zero. Few other shrubs will do that. They are, however, gaudy: Some of the Northern Lights azaleas, if their colors were used in clothing, would be suitable for road workers wishing to avoid being hit by traffic.

Some Lesser-Known Shrubs

If your taste turns to something different, Steve Sweedler, the horticulturist at Plymouth State University, recommends the following five woodies.

Pieris **'Brouwer's Beauty':** Zone 5; 4 to 6 feet. Small and delicate, this hybrid's flower buds are handsome from fall through winter, producing fragrant white sprays of flowers in early spring. Mountain pieris (*P. floribunda*) stays small and blooms for a long time.

Witch hazel (*Hamamelis* x *intermedia* 'Arnold Promise'): Zone 5; 15 to 20 feet. Lacy yellow flowers with red accents in late winter.

Winterberry (*Ilex verticillata* 'Red Sprite' or 'Winter Red'): Zone 3; 4 to 6 feet. These are our native deciduous hollies; they produce red berries that shine on snow. They like wet places, and need a male such as 'Jim Dandy' for pollination.

Mountain laurel (*Kalmia latifolia*): Zone 4; 7 to 15 feet. Sweedler recommends the Jaynes hybrids for their colors—pink, white, reds—and nice evergreen leaves. 'Sarah', 'Olympic Fire', and 'Carol' are his favorites.

Viburnums of all sorts, but particularly Koreanspice viburnum (*V. carlesii*). Zone 4 or 5; 5 to 8 feet. Sweedler loves this one for the fragrance of its flowers that are pink to red in bud, opening to white. Unfortunately, there is an alien beetle that is devastating viburnums in some parts of the state. The beetles are present in my area, so I am not planting any viburnums at this time. Ask at your garden center to determine if there is a problem in your part of the state before planting viburnums.

Final Thoughts

Before you buy a tree or shrub, go look at a mature specimen. By seeing mature trees, you will have a better idea of how much space you need for each. Don't crowd your trees! Talk to a friend who has one or a knowledgeable salesperson at the nursery. Find out what that particular species needs for sun, drainage, and soil type. Read up on it—see a list of books in chapter 12.

I recommend buying trees only from local nurseries, not Big Box stores. The big stores can sell trees cheaper, but most are grown down South and may not be as hardy here as trees grown in New England. A local family-run nursery won't sell you something that is only marginally hardy in New Hampshire, or not without warning you.

Lastly, be patient. Buy a nice tree, prune it carefully each year to maintain a nice shape, and rejoice in watching it grow up —just as you do with your children.

Lawns

Almost every house in New Hampshire has a lawn of some sort, and having a good lawn means being a gardener—whether you recognize it or not. A lawn is not a green carpet that grows. A lawn is made up of millions of plants, growing, competing with each other, being stepped on, watered (or not), and sometimes getting applications of fertilizer, fungicides, herbicides and insecticides.

Chemical companies have done an excellent job of convincing many of us that lawns should look just so: short, uniform, weed free, deep green. No dandelions, no crabgrass, no clover. Three-step programs to "Weed-n-Feed" are heavily advertised on television each spring, I'm told. Well, think again. You can have a nice-looking lawn with much less work, much less cost, and no possibility of side effects due to toxic chemicals. You can have an organic lawn.

Spring Lawn Care

Most lawns look pretty awful in early April. The snowplows have dumped road sand and gravel along their edges. Leaves and sticks have fallen, wayward dogs have left deposits. As soon as the soil thaws completely and the lawn has dried out, it's time to rake it. If the lawn is soggy, it will compact when you walk on it, so do have patience and stay off until it's dried out.

Getting the lawn clear of debris is important. Grass will absorb sunshine better if it is not covered with dirt or leaves. Fertilizer and compost will start working sooner and more effectively if they are in good contact with the soil.

Despite claims by the fertilizer industry, lawns don't need big infusions of fertilizer to wake up and get started in the spring. Many chemical fertilizers consist of soluble chemicals that will be picked up by your grass almost immediately. If a rainy week follows your weekend application, however, much of the fertilizer will wash away. If you decide to fertilize, buy organic fertilizer and apply the minimum needed. Organic fertilizers have a small amount of soluble fertilizer, but most of the nutrients need to be broken down by soil organisms and are not easily washed away. Warmer temperatures increase biological activity, hence quicker breakdown of organic fertilizers.

You can spread some bagged organic fertilizer such as Pro-Gro if you are in a hurry to help the lawn green up. But even better, I think, is to add half an inch of compost. This will not only add a variety of micronutrients, it will also introduce beneficial organisms that are lacking in your soil if you've been depending on chemicals. Just drop compost onto the lawn and rake it out.

Be gentle when you rake the lawn in spring. While the lawn is still dormant it's easy to inadvertently pull up grass. I favor an old-fashioned bamboo lawn rake, but some of the new plastic-tined rakes work well, too. To save labor I rake the mess onto an 8-by-12-foot tarp, which holds several times as much as a wheelbarrow, and drag it away.

If you are intent on having a weed-free lawn—which I am not—you can reduce the number of weed seeds that germinate by spreading corn gluten on the lawn. This is an inexpensive corn by-product sold in fifty-pound bags at garden centers and feed stores. It is important to apply corn gluten early in the season for the treatment to be effective. Do it in the time between the blooming of forsythia and daffodils in April and lilacs in May.

Don't be unrealistic: Corn gluten is not a miracle. Some weed seeds will germinate, depending on your soil conditions. According to UNH Cooperative Extension turf specialist Dr. John Roberts, 50 to 60 percent of the weed seeds in your lawn may still germinate after a single corn gluten treatment.

Brian Steinwand, who is the liaison with the golf course industry for the Environmental Protection Agency, told me that golf course managers have reported great results after using corn gluten for three years in a row. Weed seeds in the soil don't all germinate at once, so repeated use appears to be necessary.

Lawns that have been treated with chemicals in the past and have relatively little biological activity will not do as well with a gluten treatment as an organic lawn. Microbes are needed to break down the corn gluten, releasing peptides that prevent roots from getting established. Unfortunately, corn gluten will also prevent any seeds you intentionally plant from growing, too. If you apply corn gluten in the spring, you can plant lawn seeds in the fall.

Corn gluten has the added advantage of adding some organic nitrogen to the soil. Unlike chemical applications of fertilizer, it won't dissolve and end up in our water systems. It is transformed into usable forms of nitrogen and minerals over time. Corn gluten contains about 10 percent nitrogen by weight.

Spring is also the time to fill in dead spots or thin places in the lawn. Scuff up the soil surface with a short-tined garden rake and scatter seed over the surface. Flip over a lawn rake so the tines are up, then run it over the seeded area. That will mix the seed into the top quarter inch of soil. Pat it down with a tamper or a board to establish good contact between soil and the seeds, or borrow (or rent) a lawn roller to do larger areas.

It is important to keep newly seeded areas from drying out. You can spread a 1-inch layer of straw over the surface or buy a paper mulch such as Penn Mulch. The latter product comes as little pellets of cellulose that absorb water nicely. Ordinary mulch hay has seeds in it, so it's better to buy straw that doesn't. If the weather is dry, turn on a sprinkler every day until the grass is established.

Pick the Right Seed for the Job

Whether you are overseeding in the spring or starting a new lawn from scratch, buying the right seed is important. According to turf specialist John Roberts, there is no one "best" lawn seed. He recommends buying premium turf grass, not the cheapest you can get. "You get what you pay for," he says. Here are his recommendations:

1. For a lawn that requires the least work (fertilizing and mowing), choose a mix that is about 80 percent tall fescue and no more than 20 percent Kentucky bluegrass. Fescue is not as fine as bluegrass, but it is deep rooted and will survive drought and high foot traffic. Few pests will bother it. Ten percent Dutch white clover in the mix will add nitrogen naturally—so long as you add no herbicides, which will kill clover. This lawn will do okay even if you do not add fertilizers.

2. Next up the ladder of work and fertilizers is a blend that is about one-third Kentucky bluegrass, one-third perennial rye, and one-third fine-leaf fescue. Some Dutch white clover in the mix is good, too. This mix will do well with one application of fertilizer per year.

3. For folks who really want the classic look of a high-maintenance lawn and are willing to fertilize three times a year, a mix of 50 percent Kentucky bluegrass, about 25 percent perennial ryegrass, and 25 percent fine-leaf fescue should do the trick.

Don't buy pure Kentucky bluegrass, thinking you will get a premium lawn. Get a good mixture of grasses. The color and texture of bluegrass is preferred by some people, but it requires full sun and more fertilizer than other grasses. Furthermore, any monoculture—such as a pure stand of bluegrass—is more susceptible to attacks by insects and diseases.

Shady Lawns

As the trees around your house get bigger and spread more shade on the lawn, your lawn will start to lose its vigor. In addition to the shade they create, trees will spread roots farther into the lawn, stealing moisture and nutrients from the lawn. Maple trees are

Planting Sod in New Hampshire

Buying sod or having it installed is expensive. Sod is grown in farms that provide perfect growing conditions for sod to grow: just the right amount of sun, water, and fertilizer. Sod comes in densely planted rectangles that can be laid down like floor tile. The problem is that you probably won't be able to give it the same care that the sod companies do. Like a drug addict going into recovery, your sod may have some tough times at your house. I don't recommend sod, but April and May is the time to install it if you wish.

notorious for spreading their roots long distances. If the soil stays moist and is acidic, mosses will show up uninvited and stay. But be open to the idea that moss isn't all bad. You don't have to mow it, and it stays green. Don't rake it, though, as it pulls up easily.

Realisitically, you'll probably need to plant more than one mixture of grass seed on your property. For areas of shade, buy a mix that has about 70 percent fine fescue, 20 percent perennial rye-grass, and perhaps 10 percent Kentucky bluegrass of a shade-tolerant variety.

Weeds

Weeds are, by definition, tough plants growing where you wish they wouldn't. In lawns they grow where turf grasses struggle—especially where the soil is compacted. Crabgrass and weeds take over when they can outcompete the lawn grasses. Here are six suggestions:

1. Get a soil test done, then follow the recommendations. Soil pH is important and easy to fix. The ratio of calcium to magnesium is important, too. A ratio of 7:1 to 10:1 is good. Add calcitic limestone not dolomitic limestone, if there is already plenty of mag-

nesium. If the pH is right but calcium is low, add gypsum, which won't affect pH.

2. If your lawn fails the screwdriver test (see the sidebar) and you wish to take drastic action, the next step is to rent a core-aerator machine. This engine-powered machine will punch little holes in the lawn to loosen up compacted soils and to allow compost or fertilizer to get down to the roots of the grass. In small areas you can aerate with a fine-tined pitchfork. Some people wear golf spikes to aerate the soil, but that sounds silly to me. Applying compost after aerating will jump-start the recovery process.

3. Add compost each spring and fall to attract earthworms and other beneficial organisms. Half an inch will help.

4. Keep the mower blade at 3 inches. Tall turf grass will help to shade out some weeds, particularly in the spring.

The Screwdriver/ Lawn Compaction Test

Try this simple test to see if your lawn is compacted. Get a screwdriver with a 6-inch shaft and try to insert it into the soil. You should be able to push it in, using moderate force, up to the hilt. If you can't, your lawn is compacted and needs help.

5. Stop walking where the lawn is compacted and struggling. You could put down pavers or stepping-stones so that people will walk on them instead of the grass. Use a sharp knife to cut out the lawn in the shape of your stepping-stones, and set them into the lawn at the level of the soil surface. That way you can run right over them with the lawn mower.

6. Plant creeping thyme or another ground cover where the lawn won't grow. Thyme smells lovely when you step on it, and some varieties stay very low.

Summer Lawn Care

It's summertime and you will have to mow. You may need to water (though I don't) and you will need to decide how to use your grass clippings.

Mowing and Mowers

Mow the lawn when it needs it, not on a fixed schedule such as every Saturday morning. Keep the blade sharp so that it cuts, not tears, the blades of grass.

Keep the blade up as high as it will go, preferably 3 inches. Grass survives by virtue of making its own food by photosynthesis. The more leaf area, the more food a grass plant makes. The more food, the better roots it will grow. Longer, deeper roots survive droughts and stresses better and create a spongier lawn.

What type of mower works best? It depends. Sheep were the original lawn mowers, and I've tried them. I used a portable electric fence, moving it around the property every few days. But that gets old—fast. Sheep are more trouble than they are worth, despite the free fertilizer. They don't cut the grass evenly and are always trying to eat your flowers.

Old-fashioned push mowers were invented around 1830 and were the way to mow lawns for about a hundred years. The labor of pushing them encouraged people to keep lawns small. Now unless you have just a tenth-acre lot and like exercise, you probably should have a power mower of some sort.

If you have an acre of lawn or more, a riding mower is worthwhile. It doesn't make sense to spend more than two hours a week pushing a lawn mower. A riding machine can cut mowing time in half simply by being twice as wide. Generally the riders are faster than push mowers, too. A basic 10-horsepower mower will do for three acres or less, if you just want to mow. If you're interested in adding other accessories, you'll need at least a 15-horsepower mower.

The turning radius is important if you have lots of trees, rocks, and flower beds to mow around. A mower with a 16-inch turning radius can mow tight to a 32-inch diameter island, but a 20-inch radius machine will require you to back up and take a couple of tries to mow around that bed.

Watering

I never water my lawn, and it doesn't die. Like any lawn it will go dormant during long periods of hot, dry weather and lose some of its green color. That's normal. It revives after the drought. Lawns cut close to the ground will scorch and turn brown before lawns with longer grass.

It is possible to keep your lawn a gorgeous green right through August. Golf courses do it. They also water every day. A lawn needs more water as temperatures rise. A minimum of 1 inch of rain per week is needed to keep a lawn looking green in a dry period, or more than that if you wait until the lawn is parched. Sandy soils need more than clay soils. If you use a sprinkler, put out an empty tuna can

When to Water

Lawn experts agree that watering in the morning is better than in the evening. That allows the day's sun and wind to dry the leaves before nightfall, minimizing fungal problems that wet leaves can develop in hot, humid summer nights. Watering in the heat of the day just wastes water due to evaporation.

about 8 feet from the sprinkler and time how long it takes to deliver an inch of rain. Check the distribution of the sprinkler with cans elsewhere, too. After a watering, the soil should be moist down to 6 inches.

Grass Clippings versus Thatch

Lawn jockeys, the guys who ride around on huge lawn mowers for a living, are forever lamenting the presence of thatch on lawns. They want to catch every blade of grass and power rake your lawn to get rid of thatch. Don't let them.

Grass clippings that fall on a biologically active lawn, one that has not been treated with chemicals, will be broken down by the organisms in it. The clippings are rich in nitrogen, and they return that nitrogen to the soil. Grass clippings and clover in a lawn can produce enough nitrogen to keep a low-maintenance lawn looking good without fertilizers. Chemically treated lawns have a much harder time processing clippings and may accumulate thatch. If it gets to be more than a half inch thick, it needs to be raked out. Half an inch or less can act as mulch, holding in water and keeping weeds from germinating.

Pests and Diseases

A good healthy lawn shouldn't be plagued with diseases. In the spring many lawns will have what appear to be dead spots, but these generally recover without treatment. Sometimes a spring lawn will have patches of snow mold or other fungal diseases. For advice, contact the UNH Family, Home & Garden Center or call your county extension agent (see chapter 12).

Lawns that are given too much chemical nitrogen fertilizer grow fast and have weak leaves. The excess nitrogen makes grass attractive to pests and diseases. Joe Mooney, the groundskeeper at Fenway Park in Boston for thirty-five years, kept the grass under an inch long and pumped it up weekly with fertilizers. But I visited the

Henry's Magical Mole Mix

A friend of mine had a dog that dug up her small lawn because he wanted to catch the moles there. I made up a simple mixture of castor oil and soap and spread it using a watering can, and the moles packed their bags and never returned. And the dog was out of the doghouse.

Mix one tablespoon of castor oil (available at local pharmacies) with two tablespoons of liquid soap (not dish detergent) in a blender until it gets stiff like shaving cream. Then mix in six tablespoons of water. Add two ounces of this mixture to two gallons of water in a watering can. Sprinkle the diluted mixture on the lawn.

When you buy your castor oil, make sure it is the old-fashioned type, not the new, improved, descented type.

underground storehouse of fungicides and insecticides that he needed to keep the lawn healthy, and that approach is not for me.

Moles get blamed for a lot they would never think of doing, such as eating the roots of your lawn. If you have moles, it is probably a sign that you have lots of grubs—their meal of choice. You can repel them by using a commercial mole repellent, or you can make your own (see the "Henry's Magical Mole Mix" sidebar above). But if you have lots of grubs, they will be back.

Japanese beetle grubs or cutworms may live in your lawn, eating grass roots and creating dead spots if too many are present. If you think your lawn roots are being eaten by them, cut out a 1 foot square of sod, peel it back, and count the grubs. If you have more than ten, you have a problem.

A quick organic solution is to buy beneficial nematodes, a variety known as Hb nematodes (*Heterorhabditis bacteriophora* is the species). Mike Cherim of Nottingham has a business selling biological controls and explains that the nematodes will kill grubs without bothering earthworms or other beneficials. The nematodes come on a moist sponge that you immerse in water then spray or sprinkle on the lawn. He suggests applying nematodes in April, before grub larvae turn into beetles, or in August and September when the eggs are hatching. Green Spot, his company, sells enough nematodes to treat an acre of lawn for about $100 (603–942–8925 or www.green methods.com).

Cherim also says that Japanese beetles will be back to your property each year if you have roses or other things that attract them (grapes, crab apples, etc.). The long-term solution, he says, is to buy a bacterium known as milky spore. This takes three years or so to become fully effective. Of course, Japanese beetles can fly over to your roses from the neighbor's yard, but at least your lawn will not suffer from a large infestation. I asked him if our cold winters would kill off milky spore. He said no, the most likely problem would be a severe drought.

What about other insect pests on the lawn? I like Mike Cherim's attitude, especially coming from one who sells biological controls: "People are ill equipped to take on Mother Nature's role. The more you spray, the more you are taking on her role." He does not recommend using botanical insecticides like pyrethrum that are approved for use by organic farmers. They kill everything—including the beneficials—and so should be avoided.

Fall Lawn Care

September is a better time to plant grass seed than the spring, whether seeding a new lawn or filling in dead spots. Autumn soil temperatures are warmer than in the spring, and that means grasses will germinate more quickly. Fall in New Hampshire is often rainy, which also helps new lawns get established.

Limestone is very slow to move through the soil, so adding it in the fall gives it time to work its magic through winter. If you can scratch limestone into the lawn with a rake and get it below the surface a little, it will be closer to the crown, or growing point, for both roots and leaves. For new lawns, lightly rototill in limestone and compost in the top 4 inches of soil.

Mow less often in the fall as the lawn slows down. But the last two mowings should be a little shorter. In late October reduce blade height by ½ inch, then do that again for the final mowing. Long grass can get matted down by winter snows and thus be more likely to get snow mold or other fungal diseases.

Final Thoughts

Rethink your attitude about lawns. Just as Barbie dolls don't accurately portray real women, the weed-free lawns of TV ads aren't attainable without much work and too many chemicals. You would pay a lot for daffodils that would rebloom after you mowed them down. But call those cheery yellow blossoms "dandelions," and too often, it's war.

A lawn is a bit like a marriage. A good one takes some work, and it won't be perfect every day of the year. Realize that neither your spouse nor your lawn will be perfect by Hollywood standards. Accept their imperfections, and you'll be a lot happier.

CHAPTER NINE

Invasive Plants

Since ancient times, explorers have brought back seeds and seedlings from exotic lands. Some, like the apple, have been a boon to the citizens of their adoptive home. Others, like Japanese knotweed and bush honeysuckle, have been more headache than boon. New Hampshire, with its cold climate, is blessed with a natural defense against many of the invasives: our winters. Other aggressive imports have settled in and are taking over—or trying to. It is up to us, the gardeners of the state, to be responsible: We need to learn what the problem plants are, and we need to get rid of any we have growing on our property.

What makes a plant an invasive? Invasive plants are those that reproduce rapidly and take over wild habitats, outcompeting the plants that Mother Nature provided, stealing light, water, and nutrients from less-aggressive plants such as our beautiful native wildflowers. By definition invasives are alien species, plants that have come here from other countries. These plants are often good-looking plants, but they are thugs. Most invasives produce large numbers of seeds that are distributed by birds, by the wind, or by water. In most cases, invasives are nearly impossible to remove or eradicate once established, and they have extensive root systems that preclude simply pulling them up.

Back home, in their country of origin, most invasives have predators—insects or diseases—that keep their numbers in check.

Invasives may have come to the United States inadvertently in the ballast of sailing ships or have been brought by well-intentioned people who thought the plants had some commercial use. Some, like purple loosestrife, are gorgeous and were deliberately planted by gardeners.

The Official List of Prohibited Invasive Plants in New Hampshire

New Hampshire state law prohibits the following named invasives from being sold, propagated, or transported in the state. Nurseries and garden centers can be fined, and have been, for selling prohibited species. The state is not, however, forcing anyone to cut down their trees or uproot their shrubs.

Common name	Scientific name
Trees and shrubs	
Norway maple	*Acer platanoides*
Tree of heaven	*Ailanthus altissima*
European barberry	*Berberis vulgaris*
Japanese barberry	*Berberis thunbergii*
Autumn olive	*Elaeagnus umbellate*
Burning bush	*Euonymus alatus*
Blunt-leaved privet	*Ligustrum obtusifolium*
Showy bush honeysuckle	*Lonicera bella*
Morrow's honeysuckle	*Lonicera morrowii*
Tatarian honeysuckle	*Lonicera tatarica*
Common buckthorn	*Rhamnus cathartica*
Glossy buckthorn	*Rhamnus frangula*
Multiflora rose	*Rosa multiflora*
Vines	
Oriental bittersweet	*Celastrus orbiculatus*
Black swallow-wort	*Cynanchum nigrum*

| Pale swallow-wort | *Cynanchum rossicum* |
| Japanese honeysuckle | *Lonicera japonica* |

Garden plants and weeds

Garlic mustard	*Alliaria petiolata*
Giant hogweed	*Heracleum mantegazzianum*
Yellow flag iris	*Iris pseudacorus*
Japanese knotweed	*Polygonum cuspidatum*

Aquatic species

Fanwort	*Cabomba caroliniana*
Variable milfoil	*Myriophyllum heterophyllum*
Purple loosestrife	*Lythrum salicaria*
Common reed	*Phragmites australis*

Other invasives not yet on the official list

| Goutweed/Bishop's weed | *Aegopodium podagraria* |

You can see pictures and descriptions of the official list of invasive plants on the Web at http://nh.gov/agric/divisions/plant_industry/documents/InvasivesBooklet2005.pdf.

If you find prohibited species for sale, you should speak to the owner/manager; if the seller does not immediately remove and destroy the banned species, you can contact Douglas Cygan, the invasive species coordinator for the Department of Agriculture (603–271–2561; e-mail dcygan@agr.state.nh.us).

What Can *You* Do?

For starters you can learn to identify the prohibited species and eliminate them on your own land. This may not be easy for two reasons: You may *like* the invasive species and may have planted it before you knew better. Secondly, it may not be easy to eliminate—even with the use of herbicides (which I, for one, don't want to use anyhow).

The Norway maple, for example, is a lovely tree that grows fast and survives well even in urban areas. It will grow in sun or partial shade and is not bothered by road salt. If you have a Norway maple shading your house, I can understand why you might be hesitant to cut it down.

If you are a city dweller, you may assume that since there are no forests nearby, it shouldn't matter if you keep your Norway maple (or other invasive species). Doug Cygan has this response: "It's not just wind or birds that distribute seeds. Runoff can carry seeds through subsurface drainage systems to an outlet in a natural environment. Seed from your tree can end up in streams, rivers, ponds." Thus even city dwellers can make a difference, helping to control the propagation of this invasive tree by removing theirs. Think about it.

Is It an Invasive Norway?

To see if maple trees growing wild near you are Norway maples, do this simple test: Snap off a leaf at its attachment point and look at the stem. If it oozes a milky sap, it's a Norway maple. The leaves also tend to be broader and larger than sugar or red maple leaves.

Cygan also points out that some people don't believe that 'Crimson King', one of the most commonly sold cultivars of Norway maple, is a problem. It has rich red purple leaves—but these leaves are never seen in the wild. He said that all 'Crimson Kings' are clones of one plant that had a genetic mutation. But when 'Crimson Kings' produce seed, the seeds produce green-leaved progeny.

If you live in the country and have a nice hardwood forest nearby, consider the consequences of letting seeds carried by birds replant the forest. Do you want your grandchildren to know sugar maples and ash and oak? If so, think seriously about cutting down that purple-leaf 'Crimson King' Norway maple.

Control of Invasive Species

Each species of invasive has its own characteristics and recommended control methods. These methods can be grouped into the following categories: mechanical control, biological control, and chemical control.

For the average homeowner, the first method works just fine. However, Doug Cygan of the Department of Agriculture recommends an IPM (integrated pest management) approach—including chemical herbicides in small doses where other methods fail on stubborn species. Whether to use chemicals or not is a choice you will have to make. I recommend trying hard with mechanical controls: If you persist, you can beat most pest plants.

Mechanical Controls

Mechanical control means pulling up, cutting down, mowing, or blocking the sunlight from the invasive plants. Sometimes a combination of those techniques works well.

Have a patch of Japanese knotweed? Even herbicides won't kill an established patch. You can't dig out all the roots—I once talked to a guy who used a backhoe and went down 8 feet, trying to get out all the roots but couldn't. But digging out most of the roots is a good first step. It will deplete much of the stored carbohydrates the plant needs to send up new shoots.

Next? Think lawn mower. Once you have the stalks (and some of the roots) removed, plant grass seed. Mow it every week and the invasive's roots will not get recharged. Its stems will continue to grow for years, but if you mow it, you will win. If you don't want lawn there, think weed whacker. Go out there every week and think of your boss as the knotweed king. Cut him down, with a grin.

For trees and shrubs, cutting down the culprits is relatively easy. Unfortunately some will send up new shoots from their roots time and time again. If you keep after these sprouts, eventually they will use up their stored food reserves, but this can take years.

At the very least, cutting down most woody plants annually will prevent them from setting seed—the first-year growth should not produce flowers and seeds.

Nelia Sargent of Claremont has been battling invasives on her property for years, particularly buckthorn, a small tree. She found that cutting it down only stimulated dozens of new shoots from the roots. Instead, she kills buckthorn by girdling the trees. She uses a two-handed draw knife to remove the bark and cambium layer all the way around a trunk, creating a band 12 inches wide. It is important to get every bit of cambium, she explains, which means gouging it out with a chain saw or ax in concave spots. The tree will leaf out and try to survive, but after two or three years it is dead—roots and all. At that point she cuts it down and uses it for firewood. I've also heard that an easier way to kill buckthorn is to use a saw to cut rings around the trunk in two places 12 inches apart. In this case removing the band of bark is not necessary.

Pulling small trees is best. Little ones—in their first year or two—will uproot easily. With age (yours and the sapling's) it gets harder. There is a tool for pulling saplings called a Weed Wrench. I've used them, and they really work. A Weed Wrench of the proper size allows a 150-pound office worker to pull out trees that otherwise would not be possible to yank. It has a gripping mouth-like part and a long handle to provide leverage. Nelia Sargent has one and says it will pull young buckthorn, getting most of the root system. It does disturb the soil, she warns, so dormant buckthorn seeds there may germinate. Getting rid of an invasive is an ongoing, not onetime, effort.

You can look at Weed Wrenches on the Web at www.weed-wrench.com. They range in size from the mini (for trunks up to 1 inch) to the heavy, which will pull trees up to 2½ inches; they range in weight from 5 to 24 pounds, and in price from $82 to $189. This is a tool that might be purchased by a garden club or environmental group and shared among members.

Biological Controls

Biological controls for some invasives are vastly superior to other methods, including those "quick-n-easy" chemical controls. Controlling purple loosestrife is one of those cases. Purple loosestrife grows in wet areas, forming thick colonies that roust other plants and the wildlife that depends on a diverse ecosystem. The beautiful blossoms in August are wonderful. But it's an invader and was once hard to eliminate.

Dr. Richard Casagrande of the University of Rhode Island has been working on biocontrol of invasive species for many years. He told me that when gardeners hear that new species of insects have been introduced to help control invasive plants such as purple loosestrife, there is a knee-jerk reaction: "Great. And when they've finished eating the loosestrife, what's going to happen next? Will they eat my delphiniums—or my peonies?"

The process of introducing foreign insects to combat these pests is now tightly monitored. The University of Rhode Island has quarantine labs that are almost as tightly controlled as the perimeter around the White House. Here's what they do:

First, scientists look at how the invasive species performs in its native land. Purple loosestrife came from Europe in the early 1800s—probably in soil used as ballast in ships—but it is not a problem there. Why not? It evolved there, and over time some 120 species of insects learned to love it. Of these, fourteen are host specific, meaning that they eat it—but nothing else. A few of these insects were brought to quarantine labs to test the following: Will they eat related species of the target plants or plants that share a habitat? Will they attack any of our major crops such as corn, wheat, and soy?

If you've ever tried to dig out purple loosestrife, you know that it has an amazing root system that will challenge even the strongest back. Scraps of roots left in the ground will start new plants. Not only that, each mature plant produces millions of tiny seeds every year, so even if you did poison or pull one, the soil is

full of tiny
time-release cap-
sules—seeds—that
will start the process all
over again next year, and
the year after that, and so
forth. Even burning plants will
not solve the problem. But it can
be kept under control with the use of
introduced beetles.

Since 1994 beetles that eat purple
loosestrife have been successfully reducing
stands of this exotic. They reduce the numbers of
plants to around 10 percent of preintroduction levels; as the numbers of plants drop, so do the number
of the predator beetles.

Similar efforts are under way to control phragmites,
that tall reed grass that has such beautiful plumes in wetlands
and along roadside ditches. There are two varieties of phragmites.
One is a native, noninvasive type that is not common; the other is
the same genus, but a foreign species. Scientists are seeking insect
controls that would attack the invasive and leave the native variety—and are making good progress to this end.

So what can the home gardener do? First, realize that help is on the way in the form of biocontrols. Second, recognize that herbicides for plants (and insecticides for insects) ultimately don't work. Yes, you can kill loosestrife with a spray, but most grow near streams or marshes where herbicides are outlawed.

Can you buy beetles to eat up the purple loosestrife near your stream? Probably not. As organic gardeners, we have to accept that we are not in total control of the environment, and that sometimes we have to wait or endure some losses. Biological controls do work; they have made some exotic pests such as birch leaf miners into nothing more than minor annoyances. There are already places where purple loosestrife is no longer a problem. And scientists are working hard at finding safe, reliable ways to control pest species without chemicals.

Chemical Controls

There are a few new herbicides that have been approved by OMRI (the board that approves products for use by organic farmers). Matran-2 contains clove oil, and Xpress contains thyme and clove oils and acetic acid. They are most effective on young broad-leaved weeds and probably of little long-term value in killing invasives. They essentially burn the leaves, stopping photosynthesis for a period of time. They do not kill the root systems, and like any strong chemical—whether made from plant extracts or synthesized in a chemical plant—they must be used with great care. They can harm other living beings. They are most effective if sprayed when the air temperature is over 70 degrees.

Of the chemical herbicides, those containing glyphosate are thought to be the best, meaning that they kill plants well but are less harmful to other living beings. Roundup, made by Monsanto, is one brand name. These herbicides are sprayed on leaves or painted on cut stems. The chemicals travel to the root system where certain metabolic processes are shut down, killing the entire plant.

These herbicides are not without risk, despite industry claims.

In a review of the technical literature done by the *Journal of Pesticide Reform* (volume 24, number 4), more than forty studies were cited that showed glyphosate herbicides caused harm. Some of them cited genetic damage in laboratory tests with human cells as well as in tests with lab animals. Others showed a link with non-Hodgkins lymphoma, miscarriages, and attention deficit disorder. Still other studies showed damage to the immune system of fish and abnormal development in frogs.

Not only are there risks from herbicides, they also contain "inert ingredients" that may pose risks. These ingredients help a pesticide to stick to the leaves of plants or to spray more easily. But the composition of inert ingredients in a product is considered a trade secret and need not be listed on the label. Some ready-to-use herbicides are up to 98 percent inert ingredients. The review cited above listed a dirty dozen—twelve commonly used inert ingredients that have been shown to cause harmful side effects.

If you decide to use an herbicide, be sure to wear a long-sleeved shirt, long pants, and a hat. Buy a good mask or respirator to protect yourself from inhaling the product. And apply it on a day with no wind.

Substitutes

Once you resolve to rid yourself of invasive plants, you will probably want to replace them with good plants. Norway maple, barberry, and burning bush are the most commonly used invasives in the landscape. Here are some substitutues for them:

Norway maple:

Red maple (*Acer rubrum*): Zone 3; 40 to 60 feet, fast growing. Will do well even in soggy, poor soil. Red buds in the spring and red foliage in fall are nice. Ask at the nursery if the plant you buy has been grafted onto a rootstock, and avoid those that have —they sometimes fail at the graft union.

Ginkgo (*Ginkgo biloba*): Zone 4; 50 to 80 feet, medium to fast growth. Great urban tree, as it is salt and pollution tolerant. Interesting fan-shaped leaves.

Pin oak (*Quercus palustris*): Zone 4; 60 to 70 feet, fast growing. Survives well in heavy clay soils and wet conditions. Nice pyramidal shape.

Red oak (*Quercus rubra*): Zone 3; 60 to 75 feet, fast growing. Prefers well-drained soils. Nuts great for wildlife.

Barberry and burning bush:

Common ninebark (*Physocarpus opulifolius*): Zone 2; 5 to 10 feet, spread 6 to 10 feet, medium to fast growing. 'Diablo' has nice reddish purple foliage, as does 'Summer Wine', which stays smaller, about 6 feet; 'Dart's Gold' has yellow green foliage; all can be striking and have nice white or pinkish flowers in midsummer.

Large fothergilla (*Fothergilla major*): Zone 4; 6 to 10 feet tall and wide, medium rate of growth in youth, slow at maturity. White bottlebrush flowers in spring last three weeks. Exceptionally nice fall foliage colors; often each leaf is a slightly different color.

Japanese red maple (*Acer palmatum*): Zone 4; size varies from 6 to 25 feet, slow growing. In southern climates this is a full-sized tree. I have one thirty years old that is only 6 feet tall and wide. Rich, dark, wine-colored leaves.

High-bush blueberry (*Vaccinum corymbosum*): Zone 3; up to 12 feet tall and 8 feet wide, slow growing. Don't worry about birds eating your berries—let them. Grow it as a decorative shrub. Nice spring flowers, blue fruit, good fall color.

Other plants suitable as replacements in our climate can be found in *The Best Plants for New Hampshire Gardens and Landscapes:*

How to Choose Annuals, Perennials, Small Trees & Shrubs to Thrive in Your Garden, published by the New Hampshire Plant Growers' Association in partnership with the UNH Cooperative Extension. It is available by mail for $11.45 (including shipping) from UNH Publications Center, 16 Nesmith Hall, 131 Main Street, Durham, NH 03824.

Final Thoughts

A friend who prefers to go unnamed told me an interesting story. He went through his property and removed dozens of invasive bush honeysuckles. Within a year or two many native wildflowers that he had never seen on his property, including trillium, appeared—on their own.

If you are hedging and waffling while trying to decide if you will cut down your Norway maple or yank the barberry, think of it like this: Doing so will provide you with a place to plant the tree or shrub you've been lusting over for years but have not found a place for. We all have more wishes than space, so get rid of your invasives and plant something wonderful. I did, and I'm delighted to have places for new plants.

Garden
Solutions

Coping with Pests and Diseases

Healthy, biologically active soil produces healthy plants that resist disease and are less bothered by insects than plants that are stressed, overfertilized, or badly watered. But even the best gardener will face some challenges caused by insects and diseases, depending on the weather and other environmental factors. And let's face it: When the bugs come and start eating those tender leaves on our young cucumbers, or when mildew spreads all over our phlox, every one of us, organic gardener or not, has the urge to nuke the little so-and-sos with chemicals. But there are lots of ways of protecting and nurturing our precious plants without resorting to chemicals.

The Disease Triangle

Three factors are involved in causing plant diseases. There must be a pathogen, or disease-causing fungus, bacterium, or virus. Next, there must be a susceptible plant. Stressed, weakened plants are much more susceptible than healthy ones. Lastly, environmental factors that favor development of the disease must exist. If you can eliminate even one of those three factors, the disease will not develop.

Most plant diseases in New Hampshire are caused by fungi, plants that do not have chlorophyll and so can't make their own food by photosynthesis. Fungi depend on other plants for food. Mildews and molds are common fungal diseases. Contrary to popular belief, however, most fungi are not disease causing, and some have symbiotic relationships with green plants (that is, relationships that benefit both parties). For example, tree roots benefit from mycorrhizal fungi that share soil minerals with trees and get excess sugars from tree roots.

Bacteria and viruses can also cause diseases, but these are much less common.

Plants that have been given too much soluble nitrogen fertilizer (to make them grow fast) have been shown to be more disease prone than organically grown plants. Fast growth is softer, weaker, and more easily penetrated by fungi. Just as a run-down, sleep-deprived, malnourished child will get every cold or flu passing through school, plants growing in poor soil or pumped up on chemicals will fall prey to diseases more easily.

Disease resistance has been bred into many modern hybrids. Many tomatoes, for example, are bred to resist verticillium, fusarium wilt, or root-knot nematodes. Some are resistant to all three. Read your seed packets carefully or ask about the plants you are buying. If you've had problems with plant diseases in the past, get resistant varieties. Resistance does not mean your plants *cannot* get the disease or be attacked by the parasite. It is just less likely.

Environmental factors can often be manipulated to minimize problems. Certain fungal diseases can only successfully penetrate leaves if the leaf surfaces are moist, for example, so watering in the morning is better than in the evening for preventing those kinds of diseases. Dividing big clumps of flowers so that air circulates better can help, too.

Give a plant what it needs for optimum growth and the chances for success are better. Sun-loving plants should be grown in the sun. Growing them in the shade may make them more susceptible to disease.

Integrated Pest Management

University of New Hampshire Cooperative Extension takes an integrated pest management (IPM) approach to controlling and preventing plant diseases and minimizing losses to insect pests. The goal of IPM is to reduce the use of chemicals and the costs of using them. An IPM approach does not always eliminate the use of chemicals, but it seeks to promote the judicious use of chemicals (the least possible and the least toxic.) Some chemicals such as rotenone are derived from plants—and hence approved for organic gardeners—but rotenone would almost never be recommended in an IPM program because it is highly toxic and has a long residual effect.

The basic tenet is simple: Learn as much as you can about pests and diseases that affect your plants. If you can identify them, know their lifecycles, and attack them at their weak spots, you will do just fine, most years. The IPM strategy is to use the least toxic approach to any problem and to promote good growing techniques so that diseases don't take hold.

Dr. Cheryl Smith, plant pathologist at UNH, is a strong supporter of IPM for everyone. But, she notes, "if you're a lousy grower and you're not careful, it doesn't matter if you are a traditional grower, an IPM grower, or an organic grower—you'll still be a lousy grower." So do your homework and be a good grower.

Five Steps to Prevent Plant Diseases

Once a disease has affected your plants, it's generally too late to do anything about it for this growing season. According to Cheryl Smith, plants don't recover the way humans do. "Once a plant is showing symptoms of disease, it's usually too late to cure it or manage the disease," she says. "You can't get rid of most infections that are already there. We can't cure the leaves that are already spotted. Either we live with the imperfection or we 'amputate,' removing the infected parts or the whole plant."

The best approach is to prevent disease from occurring. According to Smith, this is done by growing vigorous, healthy plants that will naturally resist diseases. Her recommendations include:

1. Select resistant cultivars where possible.

2. Don't overfertilize. Too much nitrogen produces plants that are often susceptible to diseases.

3. Practice good sanitation in the garden: "Start clean, keep it clean, end clean." Many diseases overwinter in foliage or the stems of plants, so clean up the garden in the fall.

4. Remove—amputate—any diseased leaves and stems as soon as they show signs of disease. Obviously, that rule must be used with common sense. You won't want to remove all the leaves of a lilac with powdery mildew, for example. Discard the diseased material—don't put it in your compost pile.

5. Don't overreact. Many plant diseases are ugly but not lethal. Neither apple scab nor powdery mildew will kill your plant. Put up with some imperfections instead of grabbing the sprayer full of chemicals.

Remember, too, that good soil rich in organic matter will, in general, promote healthy plants. Farmers and gardeners who add compost to their soil every year swear that this helps to prevent diseases. At present it is not known if the soil microorganisms in compost produce substances that inhibit disease, if they outcompete disease-causing organisms, or if they just help plants to grow well and fight off diseases themselves.

Common Diseases and What You Can Do for Them

Powdery mildew: This is the white powder that appears on the leaves of your phlox, bee balm, lilacs, and other plants. If it has been a problem in the past, you might try some prevention:

- This fall, clean up any debris beneath the plants. Spores (fungal seed equivalents) overwinter in plant debris. Burn or put infected plants in the trash. Any spores left on the soil will probably be eaten up by soil microorganisms.

- Divide large clumps of mildew-prone perennials in the spring. Or prune to allow better air circulation. Move plants to full sun if possible.

- Avoid watering in the evening. Water is not required for powdery mildew to develop, but high humidity is a factor.

- Select mildew-resistant cultivars. A good garden center can help you select replacements for plants that become infected every year.

- If you see an outbreak starting, make a solution of one tablespoon of baking soda and a drop of liquid soap to a gallon of water, and spray. That should help to keep powdery mildew from spreading. Commercial organic sprays of potassium bicarbonate such as Milstop and Remedy can also be used safely.

Fungal diseases on tomatoes: Tomatoes often lose their lower leaves to fungal diseases such as early blight and septoria leaf spot; lower leaves turn brown and curl up, eventually spreading to the entire plant. Rotating the location of your plants each year can help, but crop rotation is not the solution it is touted to be, as spores can spread by wind or water. What can you do?

- Mulch with grass clippings or leaves. This will minimize splashup from the soil.

- Purchase resistant varieties.

- Stake or cage your plants to keep them off the ground and to allow good air circulation.

- If all else fails, and the problem greatly reduces your crop, move your garden. Select a site as far away as possible, and dig up the sod to start a new tomato patch.

Apple diseases are another common frustration for gardeners. Cheryl Smith notes that up to 90 percent of disease can be eliminated with good orchard sanitation. Apple scab is a common fungal disease that mars the skin of apples but rarely makes apples inedible. Apple scab spores overwinter on leaves under the tree, so rake up downed fruit in the fall. Black rot and canker spores overwinter in fruit, so rake up downed fruit, too; use a bamboo pole to knock off any apples that have not fallen. Rake again in the spring, then put down a layer of mulch.

Apple scab spores germinate in wet weather about the same time that flower petals fall. The warmer the temperature, the more quickly the spores can infect a tree. Fruit or buds can only be infected while wet, so pruning to open up the tree to breezes and sunshine will dry surfaces more quickly, helping to minimize infections.

Biological Aids for Disease Control

Three brands of commercially available products can be used for disease control.

Serenade is a product that contains a commonly occurring soil bacterium that has good antifungal characteristics. The bacterium, *Bacillus subtilis,* penetrates and destroys the disease spores but does not harm any beneficial insects or wildlife. Use it against powdery mildew, gray mold, early blight, bacterial leaf blight, botrytis neck rot, walnut blight, downy mildew, fire blight, scab, bacterial spot, and pin rot. It is said to stimulate a plant's own disease-fighting mechanisms as well. It is approved for use by organic gardeners and has no restrictions about when to use it or on what.

Messenger contains naturally occurring bacterial proteins that are good for increasing plant vigor and resistance to diseases. The active ingredient, harpin, was discovered by scientists at Cornell University, who extracted it from the bacterium that causes fire blight in fruit trees. It apparently stimulates plants to mount their own defenses against disease. The manufacturer recommends using it before diseases occur.

Plant Shield contains *Trichoderma harzianum,* a soil-borne microorganism that works as a biofungicide. It is used to prevent several types of root rot and also to prevent foliar fungal diseases if sprayed before the onset of diseases. It will not stop an infection once it has started.

Identifying and Diagnosing Plant Diseases

Some problems, like powdery mildew, are easy to identify. But most of the time you'll need some help.

My favorite book is *Insect, Disease & Weed I.D. Guide: Find-It-Fast Organic Solutions for Your Garden.* Cheryl Smith recommends *Natural Disease Control: A Common Sense Approach to Plant First Aid.* (See chapter 12.)

A great resource for gardeners in New Hamspshire is UNH Cooperative Extension. Even though a phone diagnosis is tough to do, the volunteers in the UNH Master Gardener Program staff a help hotline, and often someone can give you a good idea of what your problem is. The master gardeners are located at the Family, Home & Garden Education Center in Manchester and can be reached at (877) 398–4769. Volunteers are available from 9:00 A.M. to 2:00 P.M. Monday through Friday. Sometimes volunteers are busy and you have to wait, so let the phone keep ringing.

If you want a positive diagnosis of a disease, you can mail a sample to the Plant Diagnostic Lab, Plant Biology Dept., G-37 Spaulding Hall, UNH, Durham, NH 03824. For additional information on submitting samples, contact your county cooperative extension office (see chapter 12 for the list) or call (603) 862–3200. There is a $15 charge for samples submitted to the UNH Plant Diagnostic Lab. A sample consists of one or several specimens of a single plant species (one or several tomato plants would be a single sample; one tomato and one pepper plant would be two samples). All samples should be accompanied by a disease identification form available from UNHCE county offices, by phone at 862–3200, or online at http://extension.unh.edu/Agric/AGPDTS/PlantH.htm.

Environmental Problems

Not all plant problems are caused by diseases. Some are caused by environmental factors: things like weather as well as things we gardeners may have done wrong, such as putting rock salt on plants in winter. A severe drought can affect the health of trees and shrubs for three to five years, says Dr. Cheryl Smith. Plants rely on stored energy, and if they fail to thrive because of drought (or overly wet conditions), they do not produce all the energy they need for good growth and resistance to disease. Drought predisposes trees and shrubs to cankers, tip blights, and a generally weakened state. This is another good reason why you should water newly planted woody plants and perennials regularly their first year, and in subsequent years if rains are not adequate.

Smith also reports receiving examples of plants being burned by careless use of chemical fertilizers. Sprinkling a strong fertilizer around a plant and failing to mix it in to the soil can dry out tissue, even killing the plant. Too much chemical fertilizer in a planting hole can burn the roots. Plants should be watered before fertilizing to avoid burning roots.

Slugs, Bugs, and Things That Go Munch in the Night

Slugs? Japanese beetles? Tent caterpillars? Potato bugs? These are creatures that gardeners love to hate. These critters turn normal gardeners into vengeful killers. Asked for gardening New Year's resolutions, one reader of my weekly gardening column wrote, "I resolve to beat my record of killing 368 slugs in one day! Yes, I counted each and every one that fell under the spell of my garden pruners!"

Some gardeners lose their resolve and spray toxic chemicals when their roses are threatened or the striped cucumber beetles eat the first leaves of their little cukes. Don't. There is much you can do to keep insects off your plants, to repel them, or to trap them; then there are the time-honored methods: pick and drown them, or simply squish them.

I am rarely bothered by insect pests, and I have always been an organic gardener. Coincidence? Perhaps. But I attended a lecture by a research scientist at Ohio State University, Dr. Larry Phelan, who offered an explanation for what I have observed. Phelan wanted to see if organically grown plants attracted insect pests differently than those grown using conventional techniques. He collected soil from two farms that were across the road from each other. The soils were identical except for how they had been tended for the past several years. One farm was organic, the other conventional.

To reduce other variables, Phelan brought the soil to his greenhouse and potted it up in large containers. He then grew corn in containers, adding chemical fertilizers in some, fresh cow manure in some, and composted manure in others, using both types of soil for each method. When the corn was at the appropriate size, he released corn borers into the greenhouse and watched what happened.

The corn borers preferred the corn grown conventionally. Additionally, the long-term history of the soil mattered. The soil from the organic farm had higher levels of organic material in it and consistently was less attractive to the borers—even if used with chemical fertilizers.

Why should this occur? Plants evolved over millennia getting their nutrients through the soil food web, depending on the symbiotic relationships between plants and soil microorganisms, explains Phelan. Chemical fertilizers are imprecise, providing nitrogen for fast growth, but often giving too much nitrogen or providing it all at once. When a plant gets too much nitrogen, he says, the excess is stored in the form of amino acids, the building blocks of protein. This is like candy for kids or drugs for addicts. Insects can detect it and go to the source. In contrast, soils rich in organic matter provide nitrogen and other needed nutrients in a slow, steady stream—the way Mother Nature does it.

In another experiment, Phelan grew soybeans hydroponically (in water), varying the amount of nutrients present. The soybean looper preferred plants that were nutritionally out of balance. But not just nitrogen mattered. Iron, boron, and zinc levels were important, too. And of course, those elements are not present in conventional fertilizers, which offer only nitrogen, phosphorus, and potassium. Good soil enriched with compost should have everything your plants need.

Good Bugs, Bad Bugs

One reason not to use broad-spectrum insecticides, whether of botanical or chemical origin, is that they kill the good insects along with the bad. Just because a spray is approved for organic farmers doesn't mean that you should automatically reach for it. Rotenone, pyrethrum, and other sprays are touted as "safe for organic gardeners," but they will kill parasitic wasps, ladybugs, and other good insects. And many of the good insects are not at all obvious to most of us. They are often small and unobtrusive.

To attract good bugs, grow lots of flowers and even allow a few weeds. Chickweed, for example, is an early blooming weed that provides pollen and nectar for ladybugs before the aphids and other pests are available for their lunch. I grow flowers in and around my vegetable garden, and these plants attract and feed some of the insects that keep my garden relatively pest free.

Insects that devastate your crops are sometimes hard to fool or repel, explains Dr. Alan Eaton, entomologist for UNH Cooperative Extension. "Know thine enemy," he says. "If you understand the pest, its life history, it's easier to 'outsmart it.' You have to understand its weak points."

Below are some tricks for dealing with your most troublesome insect pests. You will notice that most can be dealt with using several methods.

Slugs: There is slug bait that is safe to use around pets and rated for use by organic gardeners. It's called Sluggo, and it works. Beer in saucers will catch and drown them, but they don't deserve the beer. Handpicking works. Or spread a band of wood ashes or sharp sand around young seedlings—slugs hate to crawl over it—though that treatment is only partly effective. Slugs feed mostly at night, and you may be able to trap them during the day if you put down boards for them to crawl under.

Japanese beetles: *Don't* buy those sex-scented trap bags or you'll have the entire neighborhood's beetles eating your plants. Handpick the beetles early in the morning, shaking them into a container of soapy water. I have had good luck repelling (or confusing) them by spraying Coast of Maine fermented salmon fertilizer. Garlic Barrier, another commercial product, helps, too. In either case it's harder to repel them once they have found your roses, so try to do it before bloom time. But Eaton explains that you can't necessarily just mask the odor of a plant to fool the insects.

Potato bugs aka Colorado potato beetle: Hand picking really works, you just need to go do it every day for a couple of weeks when they first appear. And look for orange egg masses on the underside of leaves. If you have a big problem every year, consider using Bt. It's a natural bacterium (*Bacillus thuringiensis*) that can be diluted with water and sprayed on plants. Bt is not a contact poison, it is a biological control that sickens the larvae. You can also cover plants with row cover until midseason.

Tent caterpillars: These guys eat at night, sleep during the day. So remove the tent and its caterpillars during the day and drop the whole mess in a bucket of soapy water. I swab it off with a rag or knock it down with a stick. The problem, of course, is that you can't reach the tents high up in trees. But even if your tree is completely defoliated, it probably won't die. I've seen trees refoliate from dormant buds after being stripped of leaves.

There is only one generation of tent caterpillars each year, Alan Eaton notes. He says tent caterpillars can be controlled with a product that is approved for use by organic gardeners, Dipel. It contains a specific bacterium strain (*Bt kurstaki*) that will control any caterpillar. It is not toxic to us, fish, birds, or other insects, though I recommend wearing a mask when spraying anything.

The hitch is that the caterpillars have to *eat* the Dipel. So you must spray it on leaves they will eat. It works better for younger caterpillars. It can be bought at most garden centers.

Striped cucumber beetles: These pests are about ¼ inch long and love to defoliate the first leaves of cucumbers, pumpkins, and squashes. I've also found them in the flowers of mature plants. Their "saliva" spreads diseases that can shorten the life of your plants, too. Now when I plant the seeds, I cover the hill with spun agricultural fabric or row covers. Reemay and Agribon are commonly sold row cover. This stuff is lightweight and allows air, sun, and moisture to pass through, but not bugs. I pin it down with special staples that come with it or weight it down with boards. I remove it when the plants start to blossom, as they need insects for pollination.

Tomato hornworms: Parasitic wasps naturally attack these ugly critters. If you see what look like grains of rice on a hornworm, leave the worm alone. Those are cocoons of the parasitic wasps.

Otherwise, pick and drop into soapy water.

Lily leaf beetles: The beetles are so pretty that you might want to use them as earrings: bright red with black trim, about ¼ inch long. Their larvae, in contrast, are disgusting—they carry their excrement on their backs to deter birds (and organic gardeners).

Dr. Richard Casagrande and his coworkers at the University of Rhode Island have introduced parasitoids from Europe—tiny wasps—that reduce the lily leaf beetle populations. The parasitoids are doing the job near test sites in Rhode Island and Massachusetts and are established at release sites in New Hampshire and Maine. In the meantime, I pick every day in season.

Plum curculio: You may not recognize the name, but this insect's larvae have the potential to virtually eliminate your fruit crop, and in some parts of the state it does. The larvae attack developing fruit (apples, plums, pears, peaches, cherries), causing up to 90 percent of the fruit to drop off the tree in late June and early July. The fruit that does stay on the tree is disfigured.

Eaton says the best approach is to spray trees with a water solution of a kaolin clay, something like Surround, after petal drop. This coats the fruit with a dusty barrier, and that changes the way the adult insects perceive the fruit so they don't lay eggs on it, or not so often. Particle film barriers like Surround can work on broccoli to keep off cabbage worms, too. It just means more thorough washing is needed at harvest time, and your crops look dusty. Unfortunately, Surround can be harmful to your lungs if you inhale it. It is available from Gardens Alive (see chapter 12).

Furry Pests

Deer, rodents, raccoons, and rabbits: They all want to help in the garden by getting rid of your extra vegetables and flowers. You don't have to shoot them, trap them, or fence them out, though those solutions do work. Our mild-mannered dog, Abby, helps to scare them away. Here are a few other possible solutions.

Deer are pests throughout the state, but often more so in towns and villages. Hunters can't shoot deer downtown, and the deer know it. There is also less natural forage, so they're hungry.

In areas of moderate deer pressure, I've had good luck repelling deer with coyote urine, which is available at garden centers. I just hung special plastic bottles (that have holes for the smells to escape) every 8 feet or so around a garden; inside each are cotton balls soaked with coyote urine. Deer are creatures of habit, so if they get the idea that coyotes are around, they'll go elsewhere, and not come back—until next year.

Another solution for deer is the electric fence and peanut butter trick. I know people who put out a single band of electric horse fence on fiberglass poles, about 30 inches off the ground. They spread peanut butter on pieces of aluminum foil, and then use clothes pins to attach them to the "hot" strand. Deer lick the peanut butter and are shocked. It's an easy solution and you can take it down while in the garden.

If the deer population density is high enough, they can't be deterred with anything less than an 8-foot fence. Fences really work. Of course, they are laborious to install and expensive. Just how much do you value your tomatoes?

Woodchucks and squirrels: I've had good luck trapping these rodents in a Havahart traps (www.havahart.com) and releasing them in the woods far from anyone's home. It's important to get the right size trap—you can't catch a squirrel in a woodchuck trap, or vice versa. For woodchucks you need one 36 inches long with a 12-by-12-inch opening; squirrels need one with a 6-inch square opening about 16 inches long. The traps are expensive; some town animal control officers will lend you one.

It's best to place a trap for woodchucks in one of their pathways near their den, if possible. Bait it with fresh fruit (apples, watermelon) or vegetables (beans are great) that they can't get in your garden at that time of year. You won't catch them with beans if you have a row of beans for them nearby.

Squirrels I catch with sunflower seeds, though I hear peanuts work, too. Cover the cage with a towel after you catch an animal so it won't freak out until you release it. I always leave them with a snack when I release them, and I won't trap them at the end of summer or in the fall after they have stored their food for the winter. Even so, I realize that trapped animals have a low chance of flourishing somewhere else and only catch them when there is a severe problem—like the year red squirrels started running into the house to steal dog food. I relocated about thirty squirrels that year and have never had a problem since. One or two? Fine. I can live with that.

Check with your local animal control officer or police department before releasing trapped animals. It may be illegal in some more-populated towns.

Raccoons: I've heard these are wily devils, but I've never had a problem with them, probably because I've always had dogs. You can catch them in a Havahart trap or scare them off with a radio with an all-night talk-show format. I'm told you actually need *two* radios on different stations to keep them away. An electric strand will work, too.

Rabbits: I've heard that fencing is the only way to be sure to protect your lettuce from Mr. MacGregor's nemesis, Peter. Use mesh with a 1-by-2-inch grid, and bury it 6 inches in the soil; it needs to go up 18 to 24 inches.

Voles and mice: Fruit trees can be killed by hungry rodents that chew bark off all the way around, girdling them in winter. Surround the trunk with ¼-inch mesh called hardware cloth. Mouse traps baited with fruit-flavored chewing gum will catch them, too.

Final Thoughts

Pick the right plant, put it in the right place. Nurture good soil, give plants good care. Clean up or remove any plants plagued with insects or diseases. These are the basics for being a good gardener. Healthy plants will resist insects and diseases better than stressed plants and survive serious attacks more often. Lastly, accept that problems will occur. We all lose plants from time to time to insects or diseases or from marauding animals, but I accept that. Mother Nature has a plan, and we can only do so much.

CHAPTER ELEVEN

Learning from Public Gardens

Looking at other gardens is a great way to learn. New Hampshire has wonderful public gardens that can teach you much: What plants survive here (books are not always right about zone hardiness), what combinations of plants look good together, and how big plants get at maturity. Not only that, public gardens sometimes have unusual plants that you might never have seen before. And visiting other gardens means you get a break from weeding and drudgery, if only for an afternoon. So invite a friend, pack a picnic hamper, and head out. Here are some lovely gardens in the Granite State that are worth checking out.

Southern New Hampshire

Pickety Place, Mason. Gardens, a greenhouse, and a gift shop surround a 1786 farmhouse out in the middle of nowhere. Its real attraction is the fact that the old farmhouse, which now houses a nice restaurant, was the model for Grandma's house in the original 1948 Golden Books edition of *Little Red Riding Hood*, illustrated and told by Elizabeth Orton Jones. The restaurant serves a fixed menu (with choice of vegetarian or standard fare) with seatings at 11:30 A.M., 12:45 P.M., and 2:00 P.M. Reservations recommended.

The gardens include a healing garden, a rock garden, a bird garden, and others. The greenhouse specializes in herbs; in season they have more than one hundred kinds of herbs, including twenty-two varieties of basil and thirteen of lavender. Be sure to notice the ancient white ash just outside the front door of the house. It is huge—perhaps 10 feet in diameter.

Pickety Place is located off Route 31 (go south from Route 101 in Wilton). At the blinking light go uphill on Nutting Hill Road and follow the signs. For more information go to www.pickityplace.com or call (603) 878–1151. The gardens are free and open to the public. Closed January to the beginning of April.

Cathedral of the Pines, Rindge. Started after World War II in memory of Lt. Sandy Sloane, who was shot down over Germany in 1944, this site provides a place for people of all religions to pray and to mourn loved ones. It serves as a memorial to all who have served our country. The focal point for me was the "cathedral" itself: a collection of 80-foot-tall white pines that have been carefully brashed (meaning that all the lower branches, up to about 50 feet, have been pruned off). Pews and a stone pulpit are present, and on a clear day there is a dramatic view of Mount Monadnock in the distance. Also included are several small flower gardens and private places to sit and think.

Cathedral of the Pines is located just off Route 119 in Rindge and is clearly signposted. For more information go to www.virtual nh.com/cathedralpines or call (603) 899–3300. The site is free and open to the public from May though October, 9:00 A.M. to 5:00 P.M. daily. Some of the paths are wheelchair accessible.

Rhododendron State Park, Fitzwilliam. This is the New Hampshire State Park system's only botanical park, comprising 2,723 acres of woodland, some 16 of which are dominated by our native *Rhododendron maximum*. The rhododendrons bloom in mid-July, at which time there is a ranger present and a fee of $3.00 for adults, and $1.00 for children ages six to eleven. It is a perfect place to bring a family: The paths are smooth and well maintained, and the rhododendrons form tunnels of foliage that give the half-mile walk a sense of entering a tropical jungle.

The park is located just off Route 119W in Fitzwilliam; follow signs. For more information go to www.nhstateparks.org/ParksPages/Rhododendron/Rhododendron.html or call (603) 532–8862 (Monadnock State Park).

The Seacoast

Strawbery Banke, Portsmouth. This site includes buildings, artifacts, and gardens of Portsmouth from the late 1600s to the 1950s. Six period gardens have been carefully re-created using archaeology, pollen and seed analysis (for the earliest gardens), and written records to obtain and grow the very same flowers and herbs used in the gardens of yesteryear. Most days there is an excellent guided tour of the gardens. Plants are well labeled, and each garden has a box with plant lists for visitors to take home.

The Sherburne Garden is on the site of a 1696 home. It includes unusual vegetables such as skirret, white carrots, and green beets, along with the herbs and greens in use at the time, including sorrel, burnet, red orach, and Good King Henry. These vegetable gardens were traditionally grown in raised beds made with planks—some of the earliest raised beds in America.

There is also a replication of a World War II victory garden that grows all the favorite vegetables of that era. The Shapiro Garden includes the plants grown around 1919 by a Ukrainian Jewish family: tomatoes, kale, parsnips, potatoes, cabbage, garlic, carrots, horseradish, and their favorite shrubs and flowers. The Herb Garden is a modern teaching garden with about one hundred different herbs, all well labeled. The Goodwin Garden is a formal Victorian garden next to an 1870s hothouse exhibit. "Mrs. Goodwin," dressed in period costume, is available to answer your questions.

Strawbery Banke is located near the Piscataqua River on 64 Marcy Street in Portsmouth, not far from downtown. Parking is available on-site. For more information go to www.strawberybanke.org or call (603) 433–1100. Admission is $15 for adults, $10

for youths (ages five to seventeen); tickets are good for two consecutive days.

Prescott Park, Portsmouth. This public park just across the street from Strawbery Banke is a site for All-America Trials. Some years up to 500 varieties of annuals are on display. It's a nice place to buy an ice cream and relax on a park bench after visiting Strawbery Banke.

Prescott Park is located on 105 Marcy Street. Free and always open to the public.

Moffatt-Ladd House and Garden, Portsmouth. Built in 1763, this large Georgian house was the home of a sea captain. As you enter the yard, you can't help but notice a huge horse chestnut tree that was planted in 1776 by Gen. William Whipple, the owner, when he returned from signing the Declaration of Independence. There is also an English damask rose planted in 1768.

The gardens are formal, flanking a 300-foot axis path that features unusual turf steps. The gardens in their present form were created by Alexander H. Ladd, who kept meticulous records from 1888 to 1895. Available for sale at the site is a transcription of his records, complete with names of plants used, measurements, and observations—a treasure for anyone wishing to replicate a garden from that period.

Moffatt-Ladd is located on 154 Market Street, a short walk from downtown Portsmouth. For more information go to www.moffattladd.org or call (603) 436–8221. Admission to the gardens only is $2.00; house and gardens is $6.00 adults, $2.50 children. Open daily mid-June to mid-October 11:00 A.M. to 5:00 P.M.

Langdon House, Portsmouth. Just a block or two from Strawbery Banke, this is the former home of the New Hampshire governor. Its main feature of interest is a 100-foot-long rose arbor, spectacular when the roses are in bloom.

Langdon House is located on 43 Pleasant Street; (603) 436–3205.

The White Mountains

Mt. Washington Resort, Bretton Woods. This spectacular old hotel has a great history: Churchill and Roosevelt met here, and the gold standard was decided upon here. Best is the view of Mount Washington and the White Mountains. There are nice plantings around the hotel, clustered around stone outcroppings. Thousands of daffodils bloom in the spring. Frosts are common in mid-June, so visit in August after the many annual flowers planted each year have had time to bloom.

The resort is located on Route 302 in Bretton Woods. The gardens are free and open to the public. For more information go to www.mtwashington.com or call (800) 314–1752.

Lost River Nature Garden, North Woodstock. Part of the larger Lost River Gorge and Boulder Caves site, this garden is a wonderful ten- to fifteen-minute walk along a boardwalk that rises and falls along a wooded area full of native plants, each with an informative plaque. The site is owned and operated by the Society for the Protection of New Hampshire Forests, a nonprofit. The woods along the boardwalk have native azaleas and rhododendrons, wildflowers, and native shrubs. Many of the plants bloom in June.

Lost River is located about ten minutes off Interstate 93. Take exit 32 and follow Route 112 east. Follow signs; it's about five miles from the traffic light in North Woodstock. For more information go to www.FindLostRiver.com or call (603) 745–8031. Open mid-May to mid-October, 9:00 A.M. to 6:00 P.M. The Nature Garden is free, but the hike through the gorge and caves is $11.50 for adults and $7.50 for children ages four to twelve.

The Rocks Estate, Bethlehem. This 1,200-acre estate was the summer home of John Glessner, the founder of the International Harvester Company. It features formal gardens designed by Frederick Law Olmsted, the father of American landscape architecture and one of the designers of Central Park in New York City. Apparently Olmsted visited the gardens every year for fifteen years to update the design. A new wild flower garden has been established, and a wildflower festival is held annually in May. Hiking trails are on-site.

The Rocks is located off I–93, exit 40, going east on Route 302. Like the Lost River gardens, this is owned and operated by the Society for the Protection of New Hampshire Forests. For more information go to www.therocks.org or call (603) 444–6228. Admission is free; the gardens are open dawn to dusk year-round.

Plymouth State University, Plymouth. Not strictly a garden, the campus has some of the best plantings of trees and shrubs available for viewing by the public anywhere in the state. Despite its proximity to the White Mountains, the university has a fine collection of trees such as the dawn redwood, yellowwood, pieris, various witch hazels, paperbark maple, camperdown elm, and katsura. Most are located near the center of the campus.

The university is located just off I–93, exit 26. For an updated guide to plants in bloom on campus—both perennials and woodies—and their uses in the garden, go to the Web site of Steve Sweedler, the campus horticulturist: www.plymouth.edu/psc/fsb/landscap/plantsis.htm.

Central New Hampshire

Canterbury Shaker Village, Canterbury. This is a museum created at the site of one of the Shaker colonies, a religious sect that is now defunct. The grounds include a nice herb garden and other plantings. Best known for their furniture and for the fact that all Shakers were required to be celibate (they adopted orphans to fill their ranks), the Shakers were the first to sell packaged seeds. The museum offers an Herbal Journeyman's Course each summer.

The museum is located on Shaker Road in Canterbury, about 20 minutes from Concord. Signs from I–93, exit 18, will lead you there. For more information visit www.shakers.org or call (603) 783–9511.

The Fells, John Hay National Wildlife Refuge, Newbury. One of the finest gardens in New Hampshire, this is the estate of John Hays, who served President Lincoln as his personal secretary. The rock garden is the most extensive in the state, and it is blessed with all the cultural conditions one could want, from full sun (moist or dry), to full shade (moist or dry). This means that the staff can grow any rock garden plant that will survive the winters— about 1,000 different species or varieties at last count. Running through the garden is a stream that feeds a bog and a small pond.

A formal garden goes around the main house, and there's a rose terrace. The stonework is impressive. In the pebble court is a redvein enkianthus, an uncommon shrub, said to be the largest in northern New England. The site also has a self-guided ecology trail and a fine collection of native wildflowers.

The Fells is located on Route 103A in Newbury, off Interstate

89 at exit 12. Admission is $6.00 for adults, $2.00 for children. The grounds and trails are open year-round from dawn to dusk and the house and shop are open June through October 10:00 A.M. to 5:00 P.M. weekends. For more information go to www.thefells.org or call (603) 763–4769.

Western New Hampshire

Dartmouth College, Hanover. The college has a fine collection of trees and shrubs, including many majestic old elm trees that the college has kept alive around the green despite the constant threat of Dutch elm disease. To do a self-guided tour, get a copy of *Forever Green* by Molly Hughes at the Dartmouth bookstore—it has descriptions, lists, and maps of the campus trees. There are trees on the campus not commonly seen elsewhere: mature yellowwood and kousa dogwoods, for example.

Dartmouth College is located 5 miles north of exit 18 off I–89, on Route 120.

Saint-Gaudens National Historic Monument, Cornish. Located in my hometown, this is one of the finest public gardens in the state. It has a magnificent view of Mount Ascutney across the Connecticut River, fine plantings, lawns, hedges, and sculpture.

Augustus Saint-Gaudens was a sculptor who lived in Cornish around the turn of the nineteenth century and who attracted a group of other artists who formed the so-called Cornish colony. His home is now owned and managed by the National Park Service. Saint-Gaudens himself designed some of the plantings, and many of the same varieties of plants are still featured in the gardens.

The gardens are formal, with reflecting pools and statuary. There is good plant diversity, so that something is always in bloom. During the summer there are free concerts on Sunday afternoon, which can be enjoyed outside on the lawn or inside the studio.

The house and garden are located at 139 Saint-Gaudens Road, off Route 12A in Cornish, just north of the longest covered bridge in the United States. For more information go to www.sgnhs.org or call (603) 675–2175. Buildings are open from Memorial Day weekend to October 31, grounds are open year-round. Admission is $5.00 for anyone over age sixteen, free for children.

Enfield Shaker Museum, Enfield. This twenty-eight-acre site offers extensive herb gardens and an inn, restaurant, museum, and gift shop. The Shaker Museum and gardens were established as a nonprofit in 1986 to preserve the heritage and traditions of a religious sect, the Society of Believers, whose members lived and worked there from 1793 to 1923.

The herb garden is a wonderful living collection of more than one hundred different herbs and flowers nicely labeled. It consists of roughly 11,000 square feet of garden, with well-tended beds of herbs for making dyes, culinary herbs, fragrant herbs, and medicinal herbs. These herbs are all documented as herbs used by the Shakers. In addition there are beds of everlasting flowers that are used in the gift shop and museum, although not all those were grown by the Shakers.

One side of the garden has some thirty different shrubs with practical uses, either for making crafts, dyes, or medicines. On the other is a dense bed of old roses. Behind the display gardens are production gardens, which provide the herbs for various teas and balms sold in the gift shop and where heirloom vegetables are grown in summer.

One of the nicest aspects of the herb garden is the bed designed to be wheelchair accessible and interesting to people who are visually handicapped. An herb bed was constructed with lumber sides so that it is about 30 inches high. This allows any visitor to touch and smell the herbs easily, even from a wheelchair. Labels are provided in braille as well as in standard type.

Enfield Shaker Museum is located on Route 4 in Enfield, right on Lake Mascoma. For more information go to www.shaker museum.org or call (603) 632–4346. Open Monday through Saturday 10:00 A.M. to 5:00 P.M., Sunday noon to 5:00 P.M., from

May 31 to October 31, and on fall weekends until December. Admission to the gardens and museum is $7.00 for adults, $6.00 for seniors, and $3.00 for children or students.

Other Opportunities

One of the best ways to see more gardens is to go on garden tours offered as fund-raisers by local garden clubs and nonprofits. Each June, for example, there is a great open garden event in Portsmouth organized by the Congregational Church. Go to www.southchurch-uu.org for updated information and dates.

Join your local garden club. Even if there are no open houses in your town, members of the club probably know about them in other towns. Check your local newspaper for garden tours in June and July.

People, Places and Plants magazine always lists garden tours for all the New England states in its early summer issue available in May. For more information go to www.PPPlants.com. The list is usually posted on the magazine Web site.

Final Thoughts

Gardening is a win-win activity. You can stay healthier by getting regular outdoor exercise and mentally active by learning about plants. Gardens provide beauty, flowers, and fresh food. Gardening need not be expensive, particularly if you save seeds and share with friends who do, too. But best of all, gardening is a great way to make and meet friends and to enjoy what New Hampshire has to offer. So put down this book and go outdoors!

CHAPTER TWELVE

Resources
for the
New Hampshire
Gardener

Gardening Questions

Family, Home & Garden Education Center

For a quick answer to a gardening question, call the Family, Home & Garden Education Center at UNH Cooperative Extension in Manchester (877–398–4769). It provides practical solutions to everyday questions for the citizens of New Hampshire. It is staffed by master gardeners, who are volunteers available to answer your questions about gardens, lawns and landscapes, household food safety and food preservation, water quality, integrated pest management, tree planting and care, backyard livestock, and more. In addition to addressing garden questions, the master gardeners offer written information, programs, or referrals on family finances, nutrition, parenting and child development, and 4-H youth development. You can get many questions answered online by going to www.extension.unh.edu and clicking on "gardening" or by e-mailing answers@unh.edu.

University of New Hampshire Cooperative Extension

The folks at your local cooperative extension office are another great resource, and they can direct you to experts who can answer your questions. Need a soil test kit? Want to send off a diseased plant or a scary bug for identification? Give your local office a call.

Belknap County: Belknap County Complex, 36 County Drive, Laconia 03246-2900; (603) 527–5475; fax: (603) 527–5477; e-mail: belknap@ceunh.unh.edu. Open Monday through Friday 8:00 A.M. to 4:30 P.M.

Carroll County: 75 Main Street, P.O. Box 860, Center Ossipee 03814-0860; (603) 539–3331; fax: (603) 539–3335; e-mail: carroll @ccunh.unh.edu. Open Monday through Friday 8:00 A.M. to 4:30 P.M.

Cheshire County: 800 Park Avenue, Keene 03431; (603) 352–4550; fax: (603) 358–0494; e-mail: cheshire@ceunh.unh.edu. Open Monday through Friday 8:00 A.M. to 4:30 P.M.

Coos County: 629A Main Street, Lancaster 03584-9612; (603) 788–4961; fax: (603) 788–3629; e-mail: coos@ceunh.unh.edu. Open Monday through Friday 8:00 A.M. to 4:00 P.M.

Grafton County: 1930s Nursing Home Building, First Floor, 3855 Dartmouth College Highway, Box 5, North Haverhill, NH 03774-4909; (603) 787–6944; fax: (603) 787–2009; e-mail: grafton@ceunh.unh.edu. Open Monday through Friday 8:00 A.M. to 4:00 P.M.

Hillsborough County: 329 Mast Road, Goffstown 03045; (603) 641–6060; fax: (603) 645–5252; e-mail: hillsborough@ ceunh.unh.edu. Open Monday through Friday 8:00 A.M. to 4:30 P.M.

Merrimack County: 315 Daniel Webster Highway, Boscawen 03303; (603) 225–5505 or (603) 796–2151; fax: (603) 796–2271;

e-mail: merrimack@ceunh.unh.edu. Open Monday through Friday 8:00 A.M. to 4:00 P.M.

Rockingham County: 113 North Road, Brentwood 03833-6623; (603) 679–5616; fax: (603) 679–8070; e-mail: rockingham@ ceunh .unh.edu. Open Monday through Friday 8:30 A.M. to 4:30 P.M.

Strafford County: 259 County Farm Road, Unit 5, Dover 03820-6015; (603) 749–4445; fax: (603) 743–3431; e-mail: strafford@ ceunh.unh.org. Open Monday through Friday 8:00 A.M. to 4:30 P.M.

Sullivan County: 24 Main Street, Newport 03773; (603) 863–9200; fax: (603) 863–4730; e-mail: sullivan@ceunh.unh.edu. Open Monday through Friday 8:00 A.M. to 4:30 P.M.

Plant Diagnostic Lab at UNH

If you want a positive diagnosis of a plant disease, you can mail a sample to the Plant Diagnostic Lab, Plant Biology Dept., G-37 Spaulding Hall, UNH, Durham 03824. For additional information on submitting samples, contact your county cooperative extension office or call (603) 862–3200. There is a $15 charge for samples submitted to the UNH Plant Diagnostic Lab. A sample consists of one or several specimens of a single plant species (one or several tomato plants would be a single sample; one tomato and one pepper plant would be two samples). All samples should be accompanied by a disease identification form available at UNHCE county offices, by calling 862–3200, or online at http://extension.unh.edu/Agric/ AGPDTS/ PlantH.htm.

Soil Tests

Call your local extension office or call Cheryl Estabrooke, administrative assistant in the Soil Testing Lab at UNH: (603) 862–3200. Or e-mail Soil.Testing@unh.edu. Forms can be downloaded from http://extension.unh.edu/Agric/AGPDTS/SoilTest.htm.

Soil Maps

Each county has an office of the National Resource Conservation Service (NRCS) that offers soil maps, weather information, and soil surveys. Call your UNH County Extension office, and they will tell you whom to call. The people at NRCS are uniformly helpful. You can also see information gleamed from these soil maps at http://soils.usda.gov.

Books

Every gardener needs books as references. Here are my recommendations—look through these and decide which you need. A few are pretty expensive, but you can encourage your library to get them. I've put an asterisk next to the ones *everyone* should have, while the others are for gardeners with specific interests. Some of these are out of print, but you can get them by calling your local used book dealer. Also note: Many of these authors have written several books, and generally if one is good, all are good.

Armitage, Allan. *Armitage's Garden Perennials: A Garden Encyclopedia*. This species-by-species book includes a dozen different cultivars of each of the flowers illustrated with excellent photos.

Barnes and Noble Books. *Botanica: The Illustrated Encyclopedia of Over 10,000 Garden Plants and How to Cultivate Them*. One paragraph and a photo for most common and many uncommon plants.

Brickel, Christopher, and Judith D. Zuk. *The American Horticultural Society A–Z Encyclopedia of Garden Plants*. Similar to the book above, it has a little about most plants.

*Cebenko, Jill Jesiolowski, and Deborah L. Martin, eds. *Insect, Disease & Weed I.D. Guide: Find-It-Fast Organic Solutions for Your Garden*. This wonderful book not only identifies problems but also provides life cycles and solutions. Excellent.

*Cruso, Thalassa. *Making Things Grow: A Practical Guide for the Indoor Gardener*. The best book I've seen about growing houseplants. Currently out of print, but worth looking for secondhand.

Dirr, Michael. *Dirr's Hardy Trees and Shrubs: An Illustrated Encyclopedia*. The perfect companion to his book listed next, it is full of excellent photos. It's a great book to thumb through before going to the plant nursery.

Dirr, Michael. *Manual of Woody Landscape Plants: Their Identification, Ornamental Characteristics, Culture, Propagation and Uses*. This is my bible for woody plants. Dirr is the most knowledgeable author about trees. He is also highly opinionated. His book is an $80 paperback with 1,200 pages of useful information. Your local library should have it or be able to get it through interlibrary loan.

*Disabato-Aust, Tracy. *The Well-Tended Perennial Garden: Planting and Pruning Techniques*. This is a must-have because it will tell you when and how to prune your perennials for better vigor—and how to get them to bloom more than once a season.

Eddison, Sydney. *The Gardener's Palette: Creating Color in the Garden*. This explains how colors work and how to combine them. Great design tips.

Hanson, Beth, ed. *Natural Disease Control: A Common Sense Approach to Plant First Aid*. Published by the Brooklyn Botanical Gardens, this book is recommended by Dr. Cheryl Smith, plant pathologist at UNH.

Hayward, Gordon. *Stone in the Garden: Inspiring Designs and Practical Projects*. Hayward is a Vermont-based garden designer whose books are all excellent. This one is for anyone who needs to build a wall or a walk.

Hill, Lewis, and Nancy Hill. *The Flower Gardener's Bible*. The Hills are Vermonters who have been in the nursery business for fifty years or more, and all their books are excellent. This starts with the soil, covers design issues, and includes a plant-by-plant directory with pictures.

Hodgson, Larry. *Annuals for Every Purpose: Choosing the Right Plants for Your Conditions, Your Garden, and Your Taste*. There are too many annuals to know them all, but these guy seems to. A Rodale book, so it has an organic slant to flower care.

*Homeyer, Henry. *Notes from the Garden: Reflections and Observations of an Organic Gardener*. This is a month-by month guide to what I do in my own gardens, along with interviews of interesting gardeners. Selected as one of the best gardening books of 2002 by the *Christian Science Monitor*, so I'm not just bragging!

Messervy, Julie Moir. *The Inward Garden: Creating a Place of Beauty and Meaning*. An excellent book to help you understand what type of garden suits you best and how to create it.

New Hampshire Plant Growers' Association in Partnership with UNH Cooperative Extension. *The Best Plants for New Hampshire Gardens and Landscapes: How to Choose Annuals, Perennials, Small Trees & Shrubs to Thrive in Your Garden*. The title says it all.

Ogren, Thomas. *Allergy-Free Gardening: The Revolutionary Guide to Healthy Landscaping*. Useful for anyone who suffers from pollen allergies.

*Reich, Lee. *The Pruning Book*. This is the best book on pruning I've seen. It has lots of good illustrations, straightforward explanations, and species-specific information for trees, shrubs, and vines.

*Smith, Edward. *The Vegetable Gardener's Bible*. This has everything you need to know to be a good organic vegetable gardener. If you wish to grow vegetables in containers, his book *Incredible Vegetables from Self-Watering Containers* is excellent.

Still, Steven. *Manual of Herbaceous Ornamental Plants*. More than 800 pages of text with growing tips, hardiness zones, soil preferences, and descriptions of specific cultivars. This is the book I reach for most often, though it has only forty-seven pages of small color photos—eight per page—in the back. For the serious gardener.

Seed, Equipment, and Plant Suppliers

These are a few of the catalogs that I order from and have always been pleased with the quality of their goods. The four asterisked companies are my mainstays, but I use the others for specialty items.

Baker Creek Heirloom Seeds: These folks have a great variety of heirloom seeds—things you can't find elsewhere. The company was started in 1997 by a seventeen-year-old! (417) 924–8917; www.RareSeeds.com.

Brent and Becky's Bulbs: Excellent selection, excellent bulbs. (877) 661–2852; www.brentandbeckysbulbs.com.

Coast of Maine Fish Food: Offering products not easily found in stores. Go to the Web site (www.coastofmaine.com) and type in your zip code to find a dealer near you. The foliar fish food seems to be good for deterring many pests, from deer to Japanese beetles.

The Cook's Garden: Unusual vegetable seeds, including Kwintus pole beans, the best of all beans. Started by Vermonters and now owned by Burpee Seeds. (800) 457–9703; www.cooksgarden.com.

*Fedco Seeds: A Maine cooperative that supplies seeds, equipment, bare-root trees in season, seed potatoes, and bulbs. Prices are excellent, as is service. (207) 873–7333; www.fedcoseeds.com.

*Gardener's Supply: An employee owned company in Burlington, Vermont, that sells plants, seeds, equipment, books, and more at their retail outlets in Burlington and Williston. Their catalog has lots of good things (though not everything they have at the stores). (800) 427–3363; www.gardeners.com.

Gardens Alive: This specialty catalog provides supplies for organic gardeners, with everything from insecticidal soaps and biofungicides to red worms and composters. (513) 354–1482; www.Gardens Alive.com.

Green Spot: This company sells biological controls for gardens, including beneficial insects and nematodes to control Japanese beetles. (603) 942–8925; www.greenmethods.com.

Growers Supply: A business offering greenhouses and other supplies. (800) 476–9715; www.GrowersSupply.com.

*High Mowing Seeds: This Vermont-based company is one of the very few who sell only organic seeds. They sell varieties that do well in cold climates like ours, and they provide information to gardeners who want to save seeds. (802) 472–6174; www.highmowingseeds.com.

*Johnny's Selected Seeds: A Maine-based company that really works hard at breeding and testing plants that do well in our climate. They have developed many award-winning varieties and have an incredibly diverse catalog. (877) 564–6697; www.johnnyseed.com.

Lee Valley Tools: Very good tools at very good prices. I keep garden records in a ten-year gardener's journal the company sells, which makes record keeping easy. (800) 871–8158; www.lee valley.com.

McClure & Zimmerman: Extensive collection of unusual bulbs. (800) 883–6998; www.mzbulb.com.

New England Wild Flower Society: A great source for wildflowers, including rare ones. A visit to their headquarters, the Garden in the Woods in Framingham, Massachusetts, is a great spring field trip. (508) 877–7630; www.newfs.org.

Renee's Garden Seeds: Gourmet vegetables, kitchen herbs, and cottage-garden flowers. The seed packets are rich with cultivation information. (888) 800–7228; www.reneesgarden.com.

Seeds of Change: All certified-organic seeds. (888) 762–7333; www.seedsofchange.com.

Sprinkler Warehouse: Offering everything needed by gardeners and farmers who want to set up drop irrigations systems. (855) 290–0815; www.sprinklerwarehouse.com.

St. Lawrence Nurseries: Located in Potsdam, New York, where the temperatures reach 40 degrees below zero most years, they sell bare-root fruit and nut trees appropriate for our climate. They are fully organic, too. (315) 265–6739; www.sln.potsdam.ny.us.

Continuing Education

Master Gardener Program

The University of New Hampshire Cooperative Extension conducts master gardener training once per year, with registration in July for fall classes. If you have a flexible schedule and can commit not only to attending classes but to volunteering afterward, this is a wonderful opportunity. You can get an application at http://extension.unh.edu/Agric/documents/2006mgap.pdf or by calling the master gardener coordinator at (603) 629–9494 (ext. 110). The master gardener program offers graduates additional workshops every year.

Glossary

annual: Any plant that lives its life in one year and then dies when winter comes. Lettuce, marigolds, and crabgrass are annuals. Some flowers called annuals in New Hampshire may be perennials in the tropics.

Azomite: A commercially available rock powder that offers many minerals not found in fertilizers.

biennial: Any plant that lives just two years, then dies. Flowering occurs in the second year. Foxgloves, parsley, and carrots are examples.

branch collar: A swollen area, usually wrinkled, where a branch meets the trunk or a larger branch. It is the area where healing takes place when a branch is pruned, and it should not be removed.

brashed: To have removed all lower branches on a tree trunk, particularly those of pine trees.

cambium layer: A layer of cells in plants that is responsible for growth of the stems.

canes: Stems, particularly for multistemmed shrubs, berries, and roses.

chemical fertilizer: Fertilizer manufactured using petroleum products and chemicals.

clay: Soil that is composed of extremely fine rock particles. Clay retains water, and clay soil is commonly referred to as heavy soil.

corn gluten: A corn product sold to prevent annual weed seeds from germinating. It must be applied in the early spring before seeds germinate.

crown: The growing point of grasses.

cultivar: A named variety of a plant that has been identified as having specific characteristics. 'Crimson King' is a cultivar or variety of Norway maple that has purple leaves—most other Norway maples have green leaves.

damping-off: A fungal disease that results in young seedlings falling over and collapsing. Once it affects a plant, there is little hope for recovery.

day-neutral: A term indicating that production of flowers or fruit is not related to the seasonal changes in the length of day. Most plants do react to changes in day length.

deadhead: To cut off or remove flower heads.

deciduous: Any tree or shrub that loses its leaves in winter.

double flowers: Flowers with several sets of petals, as opposed to single flowers that just have one set of petals. Peonies and roses, for example, come as either single or double.

fungus/fungi: A parasitic plant that lacks chlorophyll and leaves, true stems, and roots and that reproduces by spores. Both beneficial and disease-causing types occur, both in the soil and on leaf surfaces. Powdery mildew, late blight, and botrytis are disease-causing fungi.

genetically modified organisms (GMOs): Organisms that scientists have developed in a lab by introducing genes from one species into another to confer special characteristics. Thus a gene from a bacterium has been introduced into a corn plant to produce a protein that is poisonous to insects, for example. Once developed, the seeds are patented and may not be saved from year to year.

glacial till: Residue deposited by glaciers, usually containing sand and rocks.

hardening off: The process of acclimatizing plants started indoors to the direct sun and to the drying effects of the wind.

hips: Seedpods of roses.

humus: A chemically complex organic material that results from the breakdown of raw organic matter by microorganisms. It is a key ingredient in all good soils, and one that makes them dark in color.

hybrid: A plant that is the result of intentional breeding, the crossing of two plants with different genetic material. Seeds from hybrids will not breed true.

hydroponics: The process of growing plants in water fortified with nutrients.

lean soil: A soil poor in nitrogen, such as an unamended sandy soil.

loam: A soil type consisting of a good balance of sand, silt, and clay.

macronutrients: Carbon, hydrogen, nitrogen, phosphorus, and potassium combine to make up the bulk of plants' bodies. All five elements are essential for plant growth and survival.

micronutrients: Elements that are important in very small amounts for the proper functioning of biological systems. Also known as trace elements.

nematodes: Small unsegmented worms found in all soils. They may be beneficial or parasitic.

nitrogen fixation: The process of taking nitrogen from the air and converting it to a form usable by plants. This is done by a few species of soil bacteria that normally reside in the roots of legumes, or bean-family plants.

organic fertilizer: Fertilizer made from natural ingredients, such as the bodies and by-products of plants and animals, and naturally occurring minerals.

organic matter: Material made by plants and animals. Leaves, manure, and seashells, for example.

pathogen: A disease-causing agent such as a bacteria, virus, or fungus.

peat moss: An organic soil additive harvested from bogs. It is somewhat acidic. It is commonly used to keep potting mixes from compacting and to retain water. It has very little nutritional value for plants.

pelletized seeds: Seeds coated with a thin layer of clay to increase their size and ability to be handled for planting. Carrot seeds are commonly offered in pelletized form.

perennial: Any plant that comes back and lives year after year. In New Hampshire perennial flowers go dormant in fall, their above-ground portions die off, and the flowers regrow in spring. Peonies, delphinium, and rhubarb are examples.

perlite: A light, fluffy material formed by heating perlite rock until it pops like popcorn. It is an inert ingredient in many planting or starting mixes. It increases water retention and aeration of soil mixes.

pH: See soil pH.

pollen-free: A term used for hybrid flowers that have been bred to produce no pollen. Pollen is usually a fine yellow dust, and it can stain tablecloths.

rock powder: Finely ground rock dust that some gardeners believe adds micronutrients and minerals that contribute to plant vigor. Ask for 200 screen rock dust if buying it at a quarry. Azomite is a bagged rock powder.

root hairs: Very fine extensions of roots that do the most important work of roots: absorbing water and nutrients. They are so small you can not see them with the naked eye.

root suckers: Shoots or stems that grow from the roots of an established woody plant. Lilacs and apples commonly send up root suckers.

scapes: Leafless flower stems. Daylily blossoms, for example, grow on scapes that can be anywhere from 1 to 5 feet in length.

silt: Soil made of medium-sized mineral particles.

single flowers: Those flowers that have just a single concentric ring of petals.

soil pH: A measure of acidity or alkalinity. It is a scale from 1 to 14, with 7 being neutral; as numbers get lower, they indicate more acidic conditions. It is logarithmic scale, so a pH of 5 is 10 times more acidic than a pH of 6. Most plants do best in the range of 6.0 to 6.8.

spores: Produced by fungi, they are equivalent to seeds in green plants.

stomata: Pores found on the underside of leaves. They are the sites where plants take in carbon dioxide from the atmosphere and give off oxygen and water.

sweet soil: Alkaline soil, or anything with a pH above 7.0. Limestone and wood ashes are said to sweeten acidic soil.

symbiotic relationship: One in which both organisms benefit. Mycorrhizal fungi, for example, share soil minerals with tree roots and obtain excess sugars exuded by the roots in return.

texture: The particular blend of soil you have, which depends on the mixture of sand, silt, and clay present.

tilth: How well a soil holds water and allows air to pass through it. "Good tilth" describes a soil that is light and fluffy.

topdressing: Adding compost, fertilizer, or manure on the soil surface near a plant to enrich the soil.

transpiration: The giving off of water vapor from the leaves of plants. Roughly equivalent to sweating (in people). Transpiration pulls up water and nutrients from the soil.

trunk flare: The base of a tree where roots flare out and appear to snake across the ground a little before disappearing beneath the surface.

variety: A cultivar. Plants that have been identified as having specific characteristics are called varieties or cultivars. Macintosh is a variety of apple.

vermiculite: A substance used to keep a planting medium light and fluffy when potting up plants or starting seedlings. It is heat-expanded mica.

water table: This indicates at what level water remains in the ground. In summer the water table might be 4 feet below the surface, but in spring there might be standing water just a foot below the surface if drainage is poor.

zones: Referring to USDA Hardiness Zones that indicate how cold it gets during an average winter. Zone 3 is minus 30 to 40 degrees; Zone 4 is minus 20 to 30 degrees; Zone 5 is minus 10 to 20 degrees. These zones determine what perennial and woody plants you can select for your garden.

Index

biological controls, 132–34
chemical controls, 134–35
mechanical controls, 130–31
New Hampshire official list of, 127–28
substitutes for, 135–137
iris, Siberian, 89

J

Jack-in-the-pulpit, 95
Japanese beetles, 124, 150
Japanese umbrella pine, 108

K

katsura tree, 109

L

Langdon House, 160
Latin names, 74
lawns, 114–25
  fall care, 125
  grubs, 123
  mowing, 120
  seed varieties, 116–18
  shady, 117
  spring care, 114
  thatch, 122
  watering, 121–22
lilacs, 109–10
lilies, 89
lily leaf beetles, 152
limestone, 15
loam, 5
Lost River Nature Garden, 160–61

M

magnesium, 12
magnolia, 108
marigolds, 73
master gardener program, 174
mice, 155
microclimates, 23–24
Moffatt-Ladd House and Gardens, 159–60
moles, 123
Mt. Washington Resort, 160
mulch, 43–46

N

nasturtiums, 75
nematodes, beneficial, 123
New England Wild Flower Society, 94, 174
nitrogen, 11, 44, 148–49
Nooney, Jill, 92

Norway maple, 129
  substitutes for, 135–36

O

open-pollinated plants, 57
organic matter, 2, 14
oxygen, 11

P

paperbark maple, 108
peonies, 88
perennials, 84–98
  bulb plants as, 95–97
  classics, 87–92
  dry hillsides and, 87
  lesser known, 92–93
  needs of, 85–87
  shade, 94
  wild, 94–95
pests and diseases, 122–24, 140–55
  animals pests, 153–55
  beneficial insects, 149
  biological controls, 145–46, 151
  common diseases, 143
  insect pests, 150–53
  lawn, 122–24
  preventing diseases, 142
petunias, 75
pH, 9–10
Phelan, Larry, 148–49
phosphorus, 11, 17
Pickety Place, 156–57
pink mallow, 91
plum curculio, 152
Plymouth State University, 161
potassium, 11, 18
potato bugs, 150
powdery mildew, 143–44
precipitation averages, 37
Prescott Park, 159
primrose, 88
public gardens, 156–65
purple loosestrife, 132–34

R

rabbits, 154
raccoons, 154
raised beds, 54–55
Rhododendron State Park, 157–58
rhododendrons, 112
Roberts, John, 115
rock dust, 118
rock phosphate, 17
Rocks Estate, The, 161